Cheap Insurance

for Your Home, Automobile, Health, & Life

How to Save Thousands While Getting Good Coverage

By Carla and Lee Rowley

CHEAP INSURANCE FOR YOUR HOME, AUTOMOBILE, HEALTH, & LIFE: HOW TO SAVE THOUSANDS WHILE GETTING GOOD COVERAGE

Copyright © 2008 by Atlantic Publishing Group, Inc.
1405 SW 6th Ave. • Ocala, Florida 34471 • 800-814-1132 • 352-622-1875–Fax
Web site: www.atlantic-pub.com • E-mail: sales@atlantic-pub.com
SAN Number: 268-1250

ISBN-13: 978-1-60138-006-7   ISBN-10: 1-60138-006-2

Library of Congress Cataloging-in-Publication Data

Rowley, Carla, 1977-
  Cheap insurance for your home, automobile, health, and life : how to save thousands while getting good coverage / by Carla and Lee Rowley.
      p. cm.
  Includes bibliographical references and index.
  ISBN-13: 978-1-60138-006-7 (alk. paper)
  ISBN-10: 1-60138-006-2 (alk. paper)
  1. Insurance--United States. 2. Homeowner's insurance--United States. 3. Insurance, Automobile--United States. 4. Insurance, Health--United States. 5. Insurance, Life--United States. I. Rowley, Lee, 1973- II. Title.
  HG8531.R69 2008
  368.00973--dc22
                          2007052809

COVER & INTERIOR LAYOUT DESIGN: Vickie Taylor • vtaylor@atlantic-pub.com   Printed on Recycled Paper

Printed in the United States

We recently lost our beloved pet "Bear," who was not only our best and dearest friend, but also the "Vice President of Sunshine" here at Atlantic Publishing. He did not receive a salary but worked tirelessly 24 hours a day to please his parents. Bear was a rescue dog that turned around and showered myself, my wife Sherri, his grandparents Jean, Bob, and Nancy and every person and animal he met (maybe not rabbits) with friendship and love. He made a lot of people smile every day.

We wanted you to know that a portion of the profits of this book will be donated to The Humane Society of the United States. — *Douglas & Sherri Brown*

The human-animal bond is as old as human history. We cherish our animal companions for their unconditional affection and acceptance. We feel a thrill when we glimpse wild creatures in their natural habitat or in our own backyard.

Unfortunately, the human-animal bond has at times been weakened. Humans have exploited some animal species to the point of extinction.

The Humane Society of the United States makes a difference in the lives of animals here at home and worldwide. The HSUS is dedicated to creating a world where our relationship with animals is guided by compassion. We seek a truly humane society in which animals are respected for their intrinsic value and where the human-animal bond is strong.

Want to help animals? We have plenty of suggestions. Adopt a pet from a local shelter, or join The Humane Society and be a part of our work to help companion animals and wildlife. You will be funding our educational, legislative, investigative and outreach projects in the U.S. and across the globe.

Or perhaps you'd like to make a memorial donation in honor of a pet, friend or relative? You can through our Kindred Spirits program. If you'd like to contribute in a more structured way, our Planned Giving Office has suggestions about estate planning, annuities and even gifts of stock that avoid capital gains taxes.

Maybe you have land that you would like to preserve as a lasting habitat for wildlife. Our Wildlife Land Trust can help you. Perhaps the land you want to share is a backyard — that's enough. Our Urban Wildlife Sanctuary Program will show you how to create a habitat for your wild neighbors.

So you see, it's easy to help animals, and The HSUS is here to help.

THE HUMANE SOCIETY
OF THE UNITED STATES.

2100 L Street NW • Washington, DC 20037 • 202-452-1100

www.hsus.org

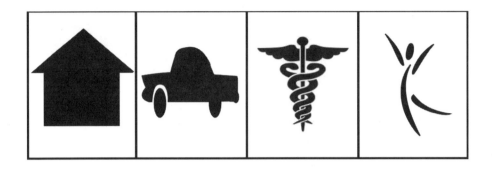

TABLE OF CONTENTS

___

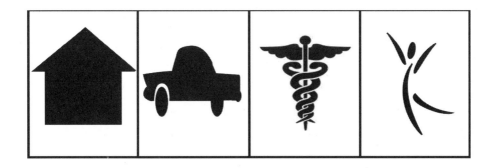

INTRODUCTION

———

In today's society, every penny counts when creating and maintaining a monthly budget. For many people, there is little room left for anything extra, and budgeting for the various types of personal insurance necessary to protect your family's financial well-being can pose a significant challenge. The cost of insurance premiums can take a large bite out of any family's budget, creating additional strain on already tight finances.

Although carrying personal insurance can be costly, it is not an expense that can reasonably be eliminated from your family's monthly budget. Failing to maintain adequate personal insurance can prove far more costly than paying premiums for automobile, homeowner's, life, and health coverage. A single accident, illness, death, or other occurrence can cost you hundreds of thousands of dollars. Without sufficient insurance, the financial consequences of any of these events could prove catastrophic.

Here are examples of the ways the four major types of personal insurance can help protect you and your family from catastrophic financial loss:

- **Auto insurance** protects you against personal liability for bodily injury or death to other drivers and damage to the property of other people arising from automobile accidents you may cause. It can also protect you against having to pay for your own medical expenses if an uninsured driver causes an accident in which you are injured. If you have a newer car, or one that could not easily be replaced, comprehensive and collision coverages pay for damage, theft, and the total loss of your vehicle.

  Also, the majority of states have passed automobile financial responsibility laws that require every driver to maintain sufficient funds to pay for damages caused to other drivers. Although some states allow drivers to place funds on deposit with the Department of Motor Vehicles to demonstrate financial responsibility, automobile insurance is a more cost-effective option for most drivers. Each year, more states pass laws that require insurance companies to report policy cancellations electronically to the Department of Insurance or the Department of Motor Vehicles. If the state receives notification that a driver's policy has been canceled, the state will require the driver to provide proof of a replacement automobile insurance policy to avoid driver's license suspension and possible fines and penalties.

- **Homeowner's insurance** protects you against substantial financial loss resulting from damage to your home, injury to a visitor while on your property, damage to the contents of your home, and loss of personal property due to theft or vandalism.

  Most mortgage companies require that you secure homeowner's insurance before the purchase of your home can be completed. The mortgage company is listed on the policy and is notified if the policy cancels. If proof of new insurance is not provided, the mortgage company will put insurance on the property and charge the homeowner for the coverage. This insurance is often more costly than if the homeowner had secured coverage from another insurance company on his or her own.

It is also necessary to carry homeowner's insurance because most of your possessions are stored in your home. If you do not carry homeowner's insurance, you may not have the financial resources available to replace your personal items or rebuild your home if damage or total loss occurs. If disaster strikes, you could be left homeless and in serious debt.

- **Health insurance** may not be required by law, but it is a necessity that can be critical to your family's financial well-being. A single illness can cost your family tens of thousands of dollars and even more if surgery or a hospital stay is required. With the high cost of medical treatment and procedures, you can be left with a tremendous amount of debt if you do not carry personal health insurance.

Do not make the mistake of thinking that if you are healthy today you will be healthy tomorrow. Even if you are seemingly healthy, you could incur an unexpected medical condition, surgery, or hospital stay at any time. By the time this unexpected condition arises, it will be too late to secure health insurance.

- **Life insurance** protects your family's finances in the event of your death. Many people assume that, if they died, their family would be able to continue paying the bills. Unfortunately, the loss of an income, along with funeral and burial expenses, can

9

place an unmanageable financial strain on the family members left behind.

Because life insurance is not required by law, it is often overlooked. This is a serious financial mistake, because it is crucial for every family to carry life insurance on anyone that contributes to the family's finances. Without the proper level of life insurance, the death of a contributor to your family's income can result in the loss of a home or thousands of dollars in debt that cannot be easily paid.

As important as personal insurance is to your family's financial well-being, it can be difficult to manage multiple insurance premiums on top of your other financial obligations. Auto insurance premiums can cost thousands of dollars each year, and health insurance premiums rise nearly every year, without providing better coverage for medical expenses. Add life and homeowner's insurance premiums to your budget, and it can cost you hundreds of dollars each month to protect your family's finances.

Fortunately, there are many ways you can save money on insurance premiums without skimping on necessary coverages, even if you have had difficulty obtaining insurance in the past. Knowing how to use these techniques will help you properly protect yourself and your family, while leaving more room in your budget for other items.

This book is the key to learning these techniques. It contains tips on how to save hundreds or even thousands of dollars each year on automobile, homeowner's, health, and life insurance and how to obtain coverage even if you have been denied an insurance policy in the past. It will also provide an overview of each type of insurance and give you tips on choosing what coverage is necessary and which ones are unnecessary.

Knowing how to save on insurance premiums will show your agent you are a savvy insurance consumer, and he or she will be required to have your family's best interests in mind when helping you select coverages, policy limits, deductibles, and policy terms.

Do not be concerned if the world of personal insurance is new to you. By the time you finish this book, you will have more insurance knowledge than 99 percent of the population. Even better, you will be on even footing with your insurance agent, which puts you in the position to obtain the best coverage possible for the least amount of money.

Before we begin exploring the four major types of personal insurance, let us start with a brief explanation of insurance and why you need it to manage the risks in your life. Understanding this will help you be better prepared when you visit your insurance agent.

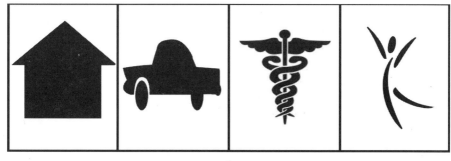

1

WHY DO YOU NEED INSURANCE?

Before you learn how to save money on the various types of personal insurance, you need to know the purpose of having insurance. This chapter will describe the fundamental reasons behind the creation and evolution of insurance and describe the applications of insurance to modern life.

AN INTRODUCTION TO RISK MANAGEMENT

There are many risks you face every single day that can affect the financial well-being of you and your family. You maybe do not spend much time thinking about these risks, because they are so interwoven into your daily activities. Here are a few examples of risks that you may face each day:

- Being involved in an automobile accident.

- Damage to or destruction of your home by severe weather.

- Death by an accident or illness.

- Injury to pedestrians while driving an automobile.

- Damage to your home caused by faulty wiring.

- An illness requiring a lengthy hospital stay.

Each of these risks carries not only emotional ramifications, but potentially devastating financial ones as well.

METHODS OF MANAGING RISK

There are several ways you can deal with each of the risks in your life:

- **Ignore the risk.** This strategy involves doing nothing to try to minimize the effects of the risk in your life. For example, if you smoke cigarettes, make no effort to manage your diet, and do not exercise, you are effectively ignoring the risk of death from heart disease. There are financial ways of ignoring the risk as well — choosing not to save enough money for your family to manage expenses and choosing not to purchase a life insurance policy.

- **Mitigate the risk.** You can mitigate many of the risks in your life through the choices you make. For example, if your family has a history of high cholesterol, you can mitigate this risk by engaging in cardiovascular exercise, limiting your intake of polyunsaturated fats, and seeing your doctor for regular checkups. You can also financially mitigate the effects of this risk by saving and investing to help your family manage finances in the event that you die or become disabled.

- **Avoid the risk.** This strategy involves eliminating a risk altogether by avoiding the places, activities, and circumstances that facilitate the risk. For most people, this is not a feasible strategy because almost any activity involves risk. Even if you manage to eliminate one risk, you are likely to create another — for example, if you refuse to drive a car because of the inherent risk of injury from an accident, you will have to take the bus or train or ride your bicycle as an alternate means of transportation. These modes of transportation create an entirely different set of risks, all of which can cause you physical injury.

- **Transfer the risk.** Transferring a risk means placing the effects of a risk on another person or entity. Most risks themselves cannot be physically transferred — you cannot give someone else your genetics or make them take your place in the hospital — but you can transfer the financial effects of risk through purchasing insurance.

Many people, particularly younger ones, tend to ignore risks — sometimes because they are not yet able to fully appreciate the presence of risk in their lives and other times because the cost of mitigating and transferring the risk seems too great. By balancing these two mechanisms, you can reduce the uncertainty that risk poses to your financial security.

As people mature, they learn to appreciate the role risk plays in their lives. They come to realize they are neither immortal nor invincible, and they begin to understand circumstances in their lives are sometimes beyond their complete control. They begin to see the need for mechanisms to properly manage the risks present in their lives.

MITIGATING RISK

There are two primary ways of mitigating the effects of risk in your life — through your day-to-day actions and through financially accounting for and preparing for risk.

Action-based risk mitigation involves taking steps in your day-to-day life to reduce the chances a risk will occur. The choices you make each day directly influence the risk of negative events that you and your family face. To reduce the chance of personal risk:

- Have the mechanicals in your home inspected regularly to ensure they are in good working order. This will reduce the risk of fire, explosion, water leakage, and gas leakage.

- Install a sprinkler system in your home to reduce the risk of the loss of your personal property, and injury or death to occupants, because of a fire in your home.

- Install a security system in your home to reduce the risk of damage to your home and loss of personal property due to vandalism or break-in.

- Make sure sidewalks and driveways are in good repair and free of snow, ice, or debris. This will reduce the risk that you will be legally liable for the injuries of a guest or passer-by on your property.

- See your physician regularly for checkups. Your physician can often identify symptoms of diseases and conditions that can be easily treated in the early stages.

- Avoid driving an automobile after drinking alcohol, taking sedatives or other judgment-impairing substances, or when you are sleep deprived. This will reduce the risk of an automobile accident, which can cause injury, death, and damage to automobiles and personal property.

- Wear a seat belt while you are in an automobile and insist that the other occupants of the vehicle do the same. Although this will not reduce the risk of a collision, it will reduce the risk of injury or death if an accident does happen.

Financial risk mitigation involves making choices to protect yourself and your family if a negative event does occur. Although this does not necessarily reduce the risk itself, it does reduce the chance that your family will be financially devastated by an illness, loss of personal property, or death of a financial contributor to the household income. Here are some of the ways you can use financial risk mitigation to protect your family's finances:

- Put a predetermined portion of your income each month into a savings account to create a financial buffer. Ideally, if your employer offers direct deposit of your pay into a bank account, you should automatically deposit a some money into your savings account and then deposit the remainder into your checking account. This will reduce your temptation to spend the money instead of saving it.

- Put your money to work for you by placing a certain amount of your income in liquid investments, such as money market accounts, mutual funds, individual corporate stocks or bonds, and Treasury securities. These investments will help your money grow while still allowing you to withdraw the funds at any time to cover a financial loss or liability.

- Place a portion of your income into higher-yield, low-liquidity investments, such as an IRA or 401(k) account. Although these investments have a higher potential for financial gain, it is not as easy to withdraw the funds. Funds placed in these accounts should be the last resource you use to cover a financial disaster, because you will incur significant penalties for withdrawing money from these accounts early. You can, however, take out a loan on a 401(k) account to cover a financial emergency, but it will have to be paid back to your account (with interest) to avoid penalties.

Although mitigating risk is important, it has limitations. From an action-based standpoint, you cannot adequately eliminate the risk of every possible loss, no matter how well you take care of your body, how carefully you drive, or how many steps you take to ensure your home is safe.

From a financial standpoint, it would be difficult for most people to place enough money in savings and investments to handle a true catastrophe. A single hospitalization can drain a savings account, even if you have $100,000 or more saved. If you cause an automobile accident, it is possible you will be legally liable for the medical expenses, rehabilitation expenses, loss of income, pain and suffering, loss of personal property, and damage to the vehicles of others. These liabilities can easily reach $1,000,000 or more if the injured people secure experienced legal representation.

For these reasons, transferring a portion of the risk is essential to maintaining your finances.

TRANSFERRING RISK

Transferring risk involves an agreement under which another person or company agrees to assume a portion, or sometimes all, of the financial risk associated with potential events in your life. The other person or company becomes legally responsible for fulfilling financial obligations you may incur as a result of an accident, illness, or death.

If you are fortunate enough to have a wealthy relative or friend, you may be able to persuade that person to agree to be responsible for financial obligations associated with your personal risks. For most people, this is not possible or practical. Transferring risk to another individual can create emotional strain between you and the other person, and it is difficult to guarantee the other person will be willing or able to meet your financial obligations should a negative event occur.

Personal insurance is the most effective way to transfer risk. In exchange for periodic payments, called premiums, an insurance company will agree to assume your financial risks, subject to limitations and exclusions outlined in your insurance agreement.

Transferring personal risk helps you plan and manage your finances because it allows you to trade a certainty (payment of insurance premiums) for an uncertainty (risk of substantial financial loss or liability). By purchasing personal insurance, you are effectively incurring a relatively small financial obligation as a means to avoid being responsible for a much larger one.

HOW PERSONAL INSURANCE PROTECTS YOU

The guiding principle of insurance is indemnification, which means that, if damage or a loss occurs, your insurance company will put you in the same financial position as if the damage or loss had never occurred.

The principle of indemnification involves determining the monetary value of losses — how much you would be financially compromised by a negative event. For example, if you walked to your garage to find that your automobile had been stolen, the principle of indemnification would hold that you would be entitled to the actual cash value of your car at the time the theft occurred.

In this example, the principle of indemnification is important because the amount you would be entitled to may be different than the amount you still owe on your automobile loan or lease or the amount you may think your car is worth because of its sentimental value to you.

You may think the principle of indemnification would hold that you would be entitled to payment for the remainder of your car's loan or lease because, if the theft had never occurred, you would not be left to pay the difference between the car's actual cash value and the amount of debt remaining on the loan or lease. However, this is not the case, because if you had sold the car for its actual cash value the moment before the theft would have occurred, you would still be responsible for paying the difference between the sale price of the car and the amount you still owe to the loan or lease company.

The principle of indemnification prevents your insurance company from being required to pay for loss amounts for which it is not responsible under your policy. This is an important function of personal insurance coverage that your insurer uses to help keep premium costs down.

Indemnification for losses and damage is subject to certain restrictions agreed on by you and your insurance company at the time the policy is written. You can use these restrictions to help further reduce your premium costs, in exchange for assuming a greater portion of the financial risk:

- **Policy limits.** You can choose the maximum amount of coverage that your insurance company will provide for a loss. For example, you could choose to purchase $100,000 of bodily injury liability on your automobile insurance policy, even though your actual liability to others may be much greater or much less. If you cause an accident in which another driver or passenger sustains $150,000 in medical, hospital, and rehabilitative expenses, your insurance company would pay the first $100,000 of the injured person's expenses, and you would be responsible for the remaining $50,000.

- **Deductibles.** You can reduce the amount that your insurance company is responsible for paying by agreeing to a deductible. A deductible is a portion of liability or damage amount that you are required to pay before your insurance company's coverage will take effect. This deductible is small compared to the policy limits — for example, you may choose a deductible of $250, $500, or $1,000.

A deductible not only allows your insurance company to manage its expenses by requiring you to retain a portion of the financial risk, but it also reduces the amount of expenses your insurer incurs for evaluating and paying claims by reducing the number of small claims submitted for payment. If your house or automobile sustains minor damage that will cost less than your deductible to repair, then you will pay for the damage out of pocket instead of submitting an insurance claim. This benefits you by keeping your premiums low, but it will also afford you additional long-term savings by reducing the number of claims appearing on your policy — your insurance company will periodically review your policy claims when determining whether to renew your policy and whether to raise your premiums.

- **Coinsurance** is a facet of health insurance policies but may apply to other types of policies as well. Coinsurance is similar to a deductible in that it allows you to retain a portion of expenses before your insurance coverage begins; however, it differs from a deductible because it is expressed as a percentage of your total claim amount rather than a fixed amount. For example, an insurance policy may carry an 80/20 coinsurance provision, which means that, on a $100,000 claim, your insurance company would be responsible for paying $80,000 of your claim, and you would be required to assume the additional $20,000.

  Under some policies, your coinsurance obligations are subject to a cap, or a maximum amount for which you are responsible per policy term. Using the example above, if your policy has a $5,000 cap per year, then you would be responsible for only $5,000 of the claim, and your insurance company would be responsible for $95,000.

Coinsurance may be used in conjunction with a deductible — if both apply, the amount of coinsurance is determined after any applicable deductible has been met. If you have a $100,000 claim with a $1,000 deductible and an 80/20 coinsurance provision, then you would pay the first $1,000 of the claim, and your insurance company would pay 80 percent of the remaining $99,000, or $79,200. In this scenario, you would be responsible for $20,800, subject to any coinsurance cap. If your policy contained a $1,000 cap, then you would be responsible for $6,000 — $1,000 for the deductible and $5,000 for the coinsurance amount.

HOW INSURANCE COMPANIES MANAGE RISK

The business of insurance involves preparing for risks that an insurance company assumes and taking steps to ensure it will be financially able to fulfill obligations that it may incur as a result of assuming those risks.

THE LAW OF LARGE NUMBERS

The most important feature of an insurance company's operations is a large amount of policyholders. Given a sufficiently large portfolio of policies, an insurance company will be able to reasonably predict the number and severity of financial losses it will be paying.

Unlike the hypothetical wealthy relative described previously, an insurance company is not only responsible for assuming your losses and financial liabilities. Instead, it is responsible for assuming the financial risk for tens of thousands of individual policyholders. By evaluating its past experience insuring individuals and paying their losses and by monitoring the loss experience of similar insurance companies, an insurer can predict its obligations over a certain time period.

Insurance companies use these predictions to determine the policy premium amounts that they will charge in exchange for assuming risks. If the actual financial obligations an insurer incurs over a specific time period are greater than the predicted obligations, the insurer will likely raise insurance premiums for the following time period.

Of course, insurance companies do not charge equal premiums to each individual policyholder. This is because individual policyholders represent different loss exposures and different degrees of risk. For this reason, insurers use sophisticated underwriting techniques to evaluate each individual risk and determine the appropriate premiums for each policy.

UNDERWRITING

Underwriting is a system of evaluating individual risks and determining if they are acceptable to an insurer. If an insurer determines an applicant poses an acceptable risk, underwriting is also used to determine the policy premiums necessary for each individual applicant.

When you apply for a policy, an insurance company may use many factors to determine whether you represent an acceptable risk and the premium amount you will pay. These factors vary by company, by the laws of the state under which your policy is written, and by the type of personal insurance you seek.

Home Insurance

- **The construction of your home.** An insurance company will consider whether your home is constructed of wood, brick, concrete block, or other material. The construction of your home affects how easily the structure can catch fire and how likely the structure will collapse because of fire or extreme weather.

- **The value of your home.** A $500,000 home represents a greater loss exposure than a $100,000 home because, if damage occurs that renders the home a total loss, the insurance company will be required to pay out a greater amount to replace the home.

- **The presence of sprinkler systems or other fire-suppressing devices.** A fire suppressant system can decrease the amount of damage sustained by a home if a fire occurs and can prevent the home from being rendered a total loss.

- **Proximity to a fire station.** The closer your home is to a fire station, the quicker firefighters can respond if a fire breaks out in your home. This can potentially reduce the amount of fire-related damage your home could sustain.

- **Proximity to a fire hydrant.** In urban and suburban areas, some insurers use this factor to determine how easily firefighters can extinguish a fire in your home.

- **Presence of a swimming pool or hot tub.** Swimming pools present a risk of injury or death to household occupants, guests, and trespassers. The presence of a swimming pool on your property significantly increases your personal liability for which your insurance company would be financially responsible. The presence of a hot tub on your property also poses the risk of fire resulting from faulty wiring or improper electrical grounding.

- **Presence of fences or other access control.** This is particularly important if a swimming pool, hot tub, large play set, or other potentially dangerous item or fixture is present on your property. Your insurance agent may make periodic visits to your property to ensure gates and other access controls are properly secured.

Automobile Insurance

- **Your age and gender.** Statistically, young and elderly drivers pose a greater risk for automobile accidents than middle-aged drivers. Likewise, male drivers pose a greater accident risk than female drivers. A few jurisdictions, such as the Commonwealth of Pennsylvania and the State of California, have passed laws that restrict or eliminate an insurer's ability to determine auto insurance premiums based on driver gender.

- **Your driving record.** The number and frequency of traffic violations and accidents can help predict your future driving habits.

- **Where your vehicle is parked at night.** This factor is based on the idea that most drivers do not venture far from home on a daily basis. Different locations represent different risks for automobile accidents, thefts, and vandalism. Some states heavily regulate the territory classifications used by insurers, helping to protect you from being grouped in a rating territory that does not accurately reflect your risks.

- **How much you drive.** Vehicles driven only on Sunday afternoons represent a lower accident risk than vehicles driven every day. Some insurers are beginning to rely on equipment installed in a vehicle, similar to a black box on a commercial jet, to verify the frequency and distance a vehicle has been driven over a policy period.

- **The age of your vehicle.** Because the value of a vehicle depreciates over time, an older vehicle is less expensive to insure than a new vehicle. This means the maximum amount an insurer would be required to pay out in the event of a total loss (the occurrence of damage that exceeds the value of a vehicle) would be less for a five-year-old vehicle than for a brand-new one.

- **The type of vehicle you drive.** Many insurers weigh the potential for damage to a vehicle and its occupants against the potential damage the vehicle is likely to cause to other vehicles and their occupants. For example, a Hyundai Accent carries a relatively low likelihood of massive damage to another vehicle but has a high likelihood of being damaged in an accident. It also provides a comparatively low level of personal protection, increasing the risk of bodily injury to its occupants.

Conversely, a Hummer H2 has the potential to withstand a collision with low to moderate damage and provides a relatively high degree of physical safety for its occupants; however, if a collision occurs, it is likely this vehicle will cause substantial damage to another vehicle and its occupants.

Life Insurance

- **Your age.** Insurance companies realize they are more likely to pay life insurance claims on older applicants than younger ones. Consequently, an insurance company will charge higher premiums on a 55-year-old policyholder than one who is 20 years old. Insurers may also place restrictions on the maximum age of an applicant at the time a life insurance policy is written.

- **Your gender.** Statistically, males are more likely to have shorter life spans and engage in risky activities than female policyholders. This increases the probability an insurance company will be required to pay on a life insurance policy for a male than for a female.

- **Your health and medical history.** Insurance companies may require applicants to submit to a physical examination, which may include collection of blood or urine samples, when evaluating an applicant for insurability. In addition, an insurer may review your medical history for indications of recurring or chronic disease. The presence of a disease or condition may cause your life insurance application to be declined or be rated at a higher premium level.

- **Your tobacco use.** Higher mortality rates are associated with tobacco users than nonusers. Insurance companies consider any type of tobacco use when determining premium rates, including cigarettes, cigars, and chewing tobacco.

Health Insurance

- **Your age.** Insurers can use your age to determine your eligibility for health insurance coverage, as well as your policy premiums, if you are accepted.

- **Medications you are currently taking.** An insurance company can use information about the medications you are currently taking to gain an understanding of health issues you may currently deal with or have the potential to incur in the future. This can affect your health insurance premiums or even your acceptability for coverage.

- **Existing health issues.** If you have an existing health condition or disease, an insurance company may use this when determining your health insurance premiums or acceptability. This is because the insurer knows that, if you have an existing health condition, it will likely have to pay for additional medications or treatment for the condition. Although insurance companies assume the risk that its policyholders will develop conditions that will require treatment, an existing condition all but guarantees the insurer will have to pay.

- **Your tobacco use.** People who use tobacco in any form have a significantly higher likelihood of developing certain conditions, such as heart disease, hypertension, and cancer, than those who do not use tobacco. Thus, an insurer can consider your tobacco use as a predictor of various health problems.

POLICY PROVISIONS

Another way insurance companies manage the risks they assume is through the language contained in insurance policies. An insurance policy is a contract between you and the insurance company that details your obligations as a policyholder and the insurance company's obligations as the bearer of your personal financial risks.

In legal terms, a personal insurance policy is a contract of adhesion. This means one party (in this case, the insurance company) drafts the language of the contract, and the other party (you, as a policyholder) accepts or rejects the terms of the contract. If you accept the terms, a policy can be issued to you, and both you and your insurer are bound by the terms of the contract. If you reject the terms, no policy can be issued, and you will need to seek insurance through another company.

In a contract of adhesion, you have no bargaining power to change the terms of the contract. The insurance company will not be willing to change the terms to meet your individual needs.

You may have accepted a contract of adhesion at least once in your life. If you purchase or lease an automobile, you signed a contract of adhesion provided by the company selling you the car and maybe another one provided by the company financing the loan or lease on your automobile. If you have a cell phone, you signed a contract of adhesion drafted by the company providing your cell phone service.

Although it may seem unfair that you have no opportunity to negotiate the terms of your contract with an insurance company, a contract of adhesion benefits you by allowing an insurer to manage a large amount of risks while keeping premium costs down. The legal resources that an insurance company would require to provide customized contracts for each policyholder would prevent any insurance carrier from being able to provide coverage at an acceptable price.

The following are the main parts of an insurance policy that an insurer uses to manage the risks it assumes.

Insuring Agreement

This section provides an overview of the contract. It states your rights and obligations as a policyholder and what the insurance company will provide in the event of a loss.

You may not realize you have obligations under the policy, but these obligations help your insurance company provide adequate coverage while managing premium costs. Typical policyholder obligations include:

- Cooperating with law enforcement officials in the event of a loss or accident.

- Notifying your insurance company of any relevant changes in your personal circumstances, such as moving to a new address, adding a room to your home, getting married or divorced, or replacing an automobile.

- Taking steps to prevent further damage to your property if a loss occurs. This may involve covering a broken car window with plastic to prevent rain damage to your car's interior or covering a portion of a damaged roof to prevent leakage.

- Cooperating with your insurance company during a claim investigation.

- Attending hearings and trials involving a damage or loss.

- Notifying your insurance company of any payments for damage you receive directly from the person who caused the damage, that person's insurance company, or other person or business.

If you were not bound by contractual obligations as a policyholder, the insurance company would not be able to effectively provide coverage for your losses. For example, if your car's window was broken but you could leave the car parked on the street with the window missing, you might expect the insurance company to not only pay for the replacement of the window, but also for water damage to your upholstery, theft of the contents of your vehicle, or theft of the vehicle itself.

Likewise, if you could receive payments from a person who caused damage to your personal property without notifying the insurer, you could end up receiving double payment for your loss. This goes against the concept of indemnification, because you would be in a better position than if the loss or damage had not occurred.

Your insurance company also has certain obligations that are stated in your personal insurance policy. These may include:

- Payment of valid claims for loss or damage, up to the chosen policy limits. In some states, insurers are required to issue payment for claims within a specified number of days.

- Representing you at trials and hearings relevant to a covered loss, even after your policy limits have been reached.

- Protecting your interests as a policyholder.

Conditions

Policy conditions elaborate on the insuring agreement and provide further information about what you and your insurance company are expected to do under the insurance policy. These conditions may address specific facets of your insurance agreement, such as:

- How claims will be paid if you have two or more policies covering the same loss.

- How your claim will be handled if you and your insurer disagree about the value of a loss or damage.

- Under what circumstances your insurance company may recover amounts it has paid to you under the policy, either from you, the person that caused the injury or damage, or the insurance company providing coverage for that person.

- The jurisdiction under which a lawsuit must be filed.

- How traveling to another state or jurisdiction will affect the amounts you can recover under your policy.

- Whether coverage will be provided for damage or losses that occur while you are in another country.

Exclusions

Although personal insurance is designed to provide you with compensation for legitimate losses, it cannot provide coverage in every circumstance. Some circumstances cannot be accurately quantified by your insurance company, which means the insurer has no way of accounting for these circumstances when determining policy premiums. Other circumstances are outside the scope of what an insurance policy is intended to provide.

Policy exclusions specifically state types of losses that will not be covered under the policy. Here are some examples of circumstances and types of losses that may be excluded under an insurance policy:

- Damage to a car that occurs while you are committing a felony.

- Damage to your home as a result of war, riot, or civil unrest.

- Death that is a result of an act of suicide. States limit the amount of time a policy may exclude suicide deaths.

- Physical injury that you incur while riding on top of a car.

- Damage to your home or car that is caused by pollution.

- Damage caused by a person acting in his or her capacity as a government official.

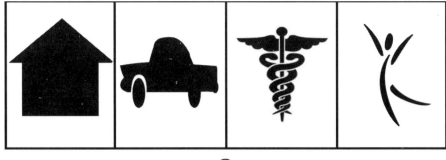

2

METHODS FOR OBTAINING CHEAP INSURANCE

It may seem nearly impossible to find cheap insurance, whether you are seeking to insure your home, automobile, life, or health. You have likely seen numerous advertisements on television, radio, and billboards for insurance companies claiming to specialize in low rates. When you call a company advertising low rates or an agent representing such a company, though, you will often find that either the company's rates are not significantly lower than those offered by any other company, or the agent will try to sell you coverage not adequate to your insurance needs. It is understandable that people become frustrated when trying to obtain insurance, because finding adequate coverage for manageable premiums can seem futile.

Whether you are new to insurance or you have purchased several policies before, there are strategies you can use to obtain cheap insurance without sacrificing the coverage necessary to protect you and your family.

COMPARISON SHOPPING

Shopping for insurance can seem a bit like car shopping — it is a task no one truly wants to undertake but is a periodic necessity of modern life. Although it is easy to take the best offer after a few calls or agent visits, perseverance can save you hundreds or thousands of dollars on your yearly insurance premiums. Here are some simple ways you can compare quotes and policy coverages available from several different insurers so that you can be sure you are getting the best deal on your insurance policy.

REFERRALS

Do not be afraid to ask for recommendations and referrals from people who already have the types of insurance you are seeking. Find out what companies they are insured through and ask for the names and numbers of their insurance agents. You will know if a friend, neighbor, or family member is happy with his or her insurance company and agent because he or she will not hesitate to put you in contact with the agent.

INTERNET SHOPPING

Another easy way to comparison shop for insurance quotes and policies is to look for insurance companies online. The Internet is a powerful resource for comparison shopping for insurance policies — more companies each year are offering online quotes to prospective customers based on information you provide. Some will even allow you to purchase policies online.

The insurance quotes you receive online are merely estimates based on the limited information you enter into the quote form. The purpose of these initial quotes is not to provide an exact representation of your insurance premiums but rather to give you an estimate without requiring you to enter several pages of detailed information. If you have entered your information honestly and have not omitted any pertinent information, your policy premiums should be within 5 to 10 percent of your initial quote.

You can also find Web sites that will allow you to enter your information once and give you quotes from several different companies. This can make comparison shopping even easier, because you can spend ten minutes entering information into a Web site form and have up to a dozen quotes and coverage plans to compare.

CONTACTING MULTIPLE AGENCIES

Although a bit more time consuming, one of the most thorough ways to compare insurance coverages and premiums is to contact nearby agencies. You can limit your time on the phone by calling one agent from each insurance company. There is virtually no advantage to calling more than one agent from the same company (unless, of course, you decide you do not like the first agent) because the agents use the same rating software throughout the company and would give the same quote.

The advantage of contacting and visiting multiple agencies is that each agent will take the time to fully explain your quote and the coverages you can obtain for different policy premiums. This method requires a greater time investment than most, but it gives you the greatest amount of information possible to make an educated and informed decision when selecting an insurance policy.

Insurance companies are required to offer quotes for free. If you are asked to pay to obtain a quote for insurance coverage, leave the office or hang up the telephone and contact your state's insurance department. The contact information for each insurance department in the United States is located in Appendix A of this book.

CONTACTING AN INDEPENDENT AGENT

Another way to easily compare premium quotes and policy coverages is to contact an independent agent. Rather than being bound to provide quotes for only one company or group, independent agents quote, write, and service insurance policies for several different companies and, therefore, can provide a quote for each company they have contracted with.

The advantage of using an independent agent is that you can obtain multiple quotes quickly. Also, since many insurance companies rely on credit scores to determine policy premiums for various insurance programs, using an independent agent gives you the advantage of having only one inquiry on your credit record, instead of having an inquiry for each company.

Make sure you keep a list of companies that an independent agent uses to provide you with premium quotes so that if you choose to visit another independent agent, or use another means to compare quotes, you do not obtain duplicate quotes from the same company.

EDUCATING YOURSELF

Another effective method for finding cheap insurance is to take the time to become educated on the coverages available on the types of policies you seek and understand what they mean. Although this will require a significant time investment, becoming educated about various insurance coverages will help you identify coverages not appropriate for your personal circumstances and keep you from declining coverages essential to keeping you and your family protected.

WHAT TYPES OF COVERAGE DO YOU NEED?

Because agents earn their livings based on commission — that is, they are paid a percentage of the premiums they write for an insurance company — some agents may try to persuade you to purchase coverages and endorsements that you may not need. Thus, it is important to discuss the quote with your agent thoroughly, so you can understand each coverage included in the quote and the reason each coverage is applicable to your personal situation. Do not be afraid to ask questions if you do not understand a coverage or policy limit or to ask your agent to explain any optional endorsements to show you how they can benefit you and your family.

ASK ABOUT DISCOUNTS

Also, make sure you are aware of the discounts that may apply — if you qualify for several discounts, you could easily cut your insurance bill in half. Agents will not always tell you about these discounts. It pays to know the right questions to ask so you can maximize your savings.

For example, if you are applying for an automobile insurance policy, be sure to check with your agent or your auto insurance company to find out if the company also offers home or renter's insurance. Purchasing both policies from the same insurance company, or through two affiliates of the same insurance company, can be advantageous to you because many insurance companies offer a special discount, often called a multiline discount.

A multiline discount can save you money on your home and automobile insurance — sometimes as much as 15 percent of the total policy premium for each type of insurance. The reason insurance companies are willing to offer this discount is because you are purchasing more than one line, or type, of insurance from them. It also benefits you to have all your insurance in one place so you can work with one agent and one company, instead of managing policies with several agents.

The multiline discount is only one of the many discounts you may be eligible for on your personal insurance. It is important to know what discounts and savings are available so that you can benefit from the lowest possible rate. This book will list available discounts for each of the four major types of personal insurance in subsequent chapters, and they are defined in the Glossary in Appendix B.

KNOW YOUR LIMIT

Before you purchase a policy or even begin the quoting process, you should have a realistic idea of how much it would take to replace all your personal property, pay off your family's bills if you passed away, or take care of your medical expenses if you became ill. Knowing how much coverage you need to put you in the same financial position as if the negative event had never occurred is crucial to your financial success because it keeps you from taking out more or less personal coverage than you need. Just remember to be realistic. Cheap insurance will not help you during a disaster if you have inadequate coverage.

You can get an idea of how much personal property coverage you need by getting appraisals on your more valuable items and by seeing what similar items cost new. You need appraisals for your more valuable items, such as jewelry and furs, because these items need to be scheduled on your policy. Your agent will most likely keep a record of the appraisal in his or her files in the event that something happens to the scheduled item.

OTHER CONSIDERATIONS

Regardless of which method you choose to compare insurance quotes, it is important to keep in mind the limits and deductibles that each company assumes when providing you with a quote for insurance coverage. For example, Company B may give you a higher price than Company A, but it is possible that Company A is quoting you at lower policy limits or higher deductibles.

It is also important to ask if your credit will be obtained as part of the quoting or application process and if it is factored into the premium quote. Some insurance companies partially base your rate on your personal credit rating and consumer reports, such as motor vehicle records, accident and claim reports obtained through the Comprehensive Loss Underwriting Exchange (CLUE), health and medical records obtained through the Medical Information Bureau (MIB), and other records and reports.

Some insurance companies run your credit and other reports at the time of the quote; others assume you have good or excellent credit and give a quote based on these assumptions. Companies that base your initial quote on information assumed by the agent or verbally stated by you will then run your credit when your agent submits your application for the policy, and you may be surprised by a higher rate.

Finally, another important thing to consider is your choice of deductible amounts for your policy coverages. Because insurance companies use different rating factors for different deductible amounts, a higher deductible means a lower rate. Make sure you know what deductible amounts your agent is basing your quote on so you have an accurate cost comparison.

Although you can easily lower your policy premium by selecting a high deductible, it is also important to be realistic when determining your deductible amount for each coverage. You should ask yourself how much you would realistically be able to pay out of pocket if you incurred property damage, a loss, an injury, or a liability for injury or damage to others. If you are not able to absorb a high deductible in the event of damage or a loss, it is better to pay a slightly higher premium for a lower deductible.

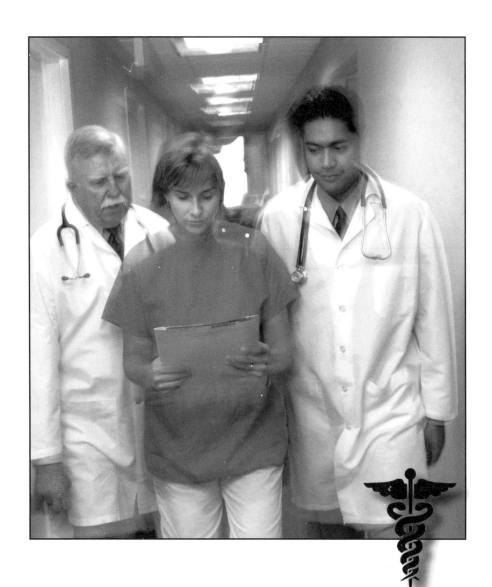

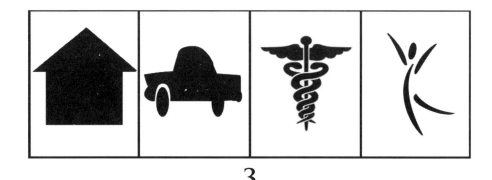

3

HOW TO CHOOSE AN INSURANCE AGENT

Finding an agent that is right for you is essential to finding cheap insurance. An effective agent will protect your interests when helping you select coverage and will stay in contact with you after you purchase your policy to make sure your coverages and policy limits are sufficient to meet your changing needs.

TYPES OF INSURANCE AGENTS

There are three main types of agents that can help you evaluate and select insurance coverage and meet your individualized needs: independent agents, captive agents, and direct writers.

Independent Agents

An independent agent is a licensed insurance provider that is not contractually obligated to write insurance solely for any one company or its affiliates. Instead, this type of agent is free to provide insurance quotes and bind coverage for several different companies. For this reason, independents can help you shop for insurance available through a variety of different companies without requiring you to submit multiple applications or travel to several different places. This is advantageous to you when seeking cheap insurance because the agent can provide you with several different quotes from competing insurance companies and help you evaluate each quote to determine which policy is best for you and your family.

In addition to helping you compare insurance quotes, an independent agent can also explain various coverage types and plans and make sure you are quoted for the specific limits and plans right for your needs. This saves you the time of having to call several different companies and compare each quote to make sure you are quoted for the same plans and limits by each company.

An independent agent is required to meet all the necessary licensing criteria set by your state's insurance laws, including pre-licensure classes, examinations, and continuing education classes. They are also required to follow the laws of each state in which they write insurance.

Captive Agents

Just like an independent agent, a captive agent is required to meet the licensing criteria of each state in which he or she writes insurance business and comply with the laws set forth by the state.

The main difference between a captive agent and an independent agent is that a captive agent has agreed to an exclusive contract with one insurance company and can quote insurance only for that company and its affiliates. A captive agent can discuss coverage limits and different policy plans with you but is limited to providing quotes for a single insurance company or affiliated group of companies.

The principal advantage of using a captive agent is he or she will likely have intimate knowledge of the products of the company or group he or she represents, so you will receive more thorough explanations of coverages and policy limitations than you would with an independent agent, who must be familiar with the policies, coverages, and insurance programs of a number of different insurers.

Direct Writer

Direct writer agents can be reached by choosing an insurance company and calling the company directly instead of searching for an independent or captive local agent. Direct writer agents are often employed by the company they work for and are not employees of a local agency. They will be able to provide you with coverage information and quotes for insurance programs offered only by their employer or its affiliate companies. A direct writer agent is also required to meet all the licensing criteria and follow the laws of the state he or she writes insurance in.

One advantage of using a direct writer agent is that he or she can often provide services over the phone, fax, and mail. This includes providing initial policy premium quotes, binding insurance coverage, taking premium payments, and assisting you with making changes to your insurance policy. In contrast, many captive and independent agents will ask you to come into their office to review the coverage and sign the paperwork, or they will ask to schedule time to come to your home to discuss insurance plans.

The primary disadvantage of using a direct writer agent is that direct writer companies sometimes experience high employee turnover, so you may find yourself working with a different agent, or a customer service representative, when you call back to make changes to your policy or make premium payments. It is important to weigh the convenience of handling your insurance needs via telephone, e-mail, or fax against your need for an insurance agent that will be there to service your policy for years to come.

WHAT TO REMEMBER WHEN CHOOSING AN AGENT

Regardless of which type of agent you choose, the most important thing to consider when choosing an agent is your personal comfort level with the person. You will not want to give your insurance business to an agent that does not set you at ease and demonstrate he or she has your best interests in mind. Here are some questions to ask yourself when choosing an agent:

- **Does he or she seem knowledgeable?** A knowledgeable agent should be able to answer any question you have, provide quick and accurate premium quotes on coverages and policies, and explain each coverage, provision, limitation, and exclusion.

- **Does the agent explain concepts in a clear manner that you can easily understand?** Because insurance agents have taken licensure classes and have passed the necessary tests to be licensed agents, they understand far more about insurance than the average person. Also, there is a certain degree of insurance jargon used between agents and agency staff that can be confusing if you are new to personal insurance. A good agent should be able to minimize the use of insurance jargon and explain things in a manner customers can understand. It should not be necessary for you to get an insurance license to understand what your agent is saying to you.

- **Does he or she seem willing to find answers to your questions, even if he or she does not have an immediate answer?** Insurance agents, while knowledgeable, do not know the answer to every question, but they should have the resources available to find the answer. If an agent cannot answer your question, he or she should show willingness to research insurance publications and materials or contact an underwriter representing the company providing your insurance policy to find the answer for you.

- **Do you feel confident the agent is going to be able to handle your policy or policies with your best interests in mind?** This requires a certain amount of trusting your own instincts because it can be difficult to objectively answer this question after meeting or speaking to your agent only once or twice. If you are not comfortable with the agent you are working with or do not feel he or she is competent to handle your policy or policies, it may be time to shop for a different agent.

AGENCY STAFF

Some agencies are bigger than others. Often, larger agencies will have a customer service staff available to make policy changes, address policy questions, and answer billing questions. Any agency staff member that makes policy changes or answers policy questions should be licensed as an insurance agent for the line of insurance your policy falls under.

In some cases, you will be working with the agency staff more than you will the agent you started the policy with. This depends on the size of the agency, the volume of business the agency handles, and how aggressively the agency is seeking new business. Here are some questions to ask yourself when you meet the agency's customer service staff:

- **Was I greeted quickly and in a friendly manner?** Agencies can be busy, but it is important an agency staff is efficient and friendly.

- **Does the licensed agency staff seem willing to answer questions?** Just like the agent who wrote your policies, agency staff members may not know the answer to every question. However, like your agent, they should demonstrate willingness to find the answer.

- **Are phone messages returned in a timely manner?** Few things can be more frustrating than leaving message after message and not receiving a return call. If you call in the morning or early afternoon, you should expect to have your call returned within the same business day. If you call late in the afternoon, your call should be returned before noon the next day.

An agency with a courteous, efficient, and helpful staff can be valuable to you because you will spend less time worrying about your insurance coverage and more time focusing on your work, family, and life.

RENEWAL REVIEWS

Many agents offer an annual or renewal review. During this review, the agent can review your policy to make sure you are receiving all the necessary coverage. Do not view this as a waste of time or an intrusion — insurance agents understand that, when circumstances in your life change, it is easy to forget that these changes may affect the insurance coverage necessary to protect you and your family.

When you go to your review, you should let your agent know of any life changes, such as a job change, marriage, the birth of a child, retirement, or change of your physical address. Any of these events can create the need for coverage changes or additional polices. For example, some companies give a savings on auto policies if the policyholder is married.

If your agent does not mention an annual or renewal review, ask if the agency currently does periodic reviews. If the agency does not, request a meeting with your agent to go over the coverages annually.

CLAIMS HANDLING

If an accident or loss occurs, an insurance agent is the first person most policyholders contact. Your agent should be able to quickly give you information about the steps you will need to take to file your claim and make sure valid claims are properly paid.

If your agent is an independent or captive agent, he or she will submit the initial claim for you so that you can focus on other aspects of your life affected by the loss, such as medical care for yourself or a family member, securing alternate shelter or transportation, or dealing with police or other law enforcement authorities.

If your agent works for a direct writer, he or she will direct you to contact the company's claims department and may put you directly in contact with an adjuster or claims processor.

Although the claims staff of your insurance company will handle most of the communication and details regarding your claim, your agent should be available to answer questions if your claims adjuster is not available or act as an intermediary between you and the company's claims staff when necessary.

The next several chapters are devoted to describing the facets of home insurance, helping you select the type of home insurance policy that is right for you and helping you find ways to save money on your home insurance premiums.

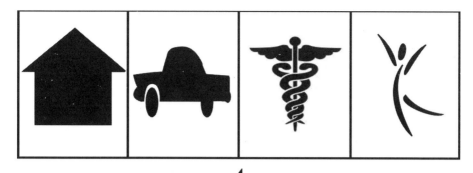

4

HOME INSURANCE

WHAT IS HOME INSURANCE?

Home insurance is personal insurance coverage that protects you against financial loss for damage to the physical belongings in your home; the residence you live in; structures not attached to your home; and mechanical fixtures in your home, such as furnaces, water heaters, and appliances. It also protects you against financial liability for the bodily injury or death of guests which arises because of an accident that occurs while the guest is on your property.

Home insurance allows a homeowner to manage personal risk by giving him or her the financial means to repair or replace damaged or stolen items and to pay for bodily injury or death sustained by guests while on the property. It can also pay for repairs to the home if it is damaged by fire, wind, hail, or any of the named hazards of the policy. This book will explain named hazards in more detail later in this chapter. If the home is completely destroyed and cannot be repaired, home insurance can cover costs of rebuilding the home and can assist you in paying for temporary housing. These coverages can help you, as a homeowner, through a situation that would otherwise be financially and emotionally devastating.

Home insurance provides coverage for disasters, such as damage caused by an aircraft, wind, hail, an explosion, riots or civil unrest, fire, or lightning. It also covers damage caused by vehicles, volcanic eruptions, theft, vandalism, smoke, and self-damaging occurrences. An example of a self-damaging occurrence would be the home collapsing in on itself.

Additions can also be made to the policy to cover further hazards, such as falling objects, water damage, snow, sleet, ice, and electrical surges. Selecting these additional coverages will result in higher insurance premiums but could prove to be worth every penny if your home is damaged or destroyed by one of these hazards.

WHY OBTAIN HOME INSURANCE?

It is impossible to foresee the future or to predict damage to your home or theft of your belongings. A home contains all your family's belongings and provides shelter from the elements, so a negative event that occurs in your home can have a profound impact on almost every facet of your family members' lives.

If damage to your home, vandalism, or a break-in occurred, it is possible you may have to replace some, if not all, of the belongings in your home. You may also have to repair or replace the physical structure of your home, which can cost you tens of thousands of dollars or more. Even if you have saved and invested a significant portion of your earnings, finding the financial resources to replace belongings, repair severe damage from fire, wind, or hail, and pay for alternate housing while your home is being rebuilt or repaired can be difficult. Without home insurance, these obligations could potentially leave you homeless and in severe financial distress.

In addition to providing resources to repair or replace your home and its contents, home insurance also provides coverage for legal liabilities you may incur as a result of injury or death to others while on your property. The liability portion of your home insurance would pay for medical expenses, funeral and burial expenses, and property damage, for which you are held legally liable as a result of events that occur on your property.

If you think you may not need to carry liability coverage as part of your home insurance because the people you invite onto your property would not hold you liable for injury or damages, keep in mind that you may also be liable for damage to people who have not been explicitly invited onto your property, such as people delivering mail, distributing flyers, or making unsolicited sales calls. In some cases, you may be liable for injuries to trespassers if you have not taken the appropriate steps to make sure these people are not permitted on your property.

These insurance coverages help reduce the uncertainty of financial loss associated with owning a home. Home insurance allows you to trade some of the financial risks of owning a home for a certain amount of periodic payment to the insurance company in the form of insurance premiums.

Home insurance may also be required by your mortgage lender before you can complete the purchase of a home. Your mortgage lender is taking a substantial risk by lending money to home purchasers, and home insurance protects these investments by helping to ensure the lender will be paid if the home is damaged or destroyed.

TYPES OF HOME INSURANCE

There are seven types of home insurance. Each type of insurance is purchased to protect the specific needs of an individual or family. Different types of homes require different types of coverage.

The first type is basic homeowner's. A homeowner's policy protects the policyholder in the event one of the events mentioned earlier occurs. It also provides liability insurance in case someone is injured on the property. Homeowner's insurance does not cover maintenance on the home.

The second type works the same as basic homeowner's but adds coverage for additional perils. This additional coverage includes water damage from water backup, snow, falling objects, and electrical damage.

The third plan provides even broader coverage. This policy would include extended and specialty items in addition to all the coverages listed above. The only disasters this policy would not cover are flood, earthquake, war, and nuclear blast.

The fourth type of home coverage is tenant or renter's insurance. This is the type of policy that would be purchased by someone renting a home or apartment. Personal property is covered against everything listed on a basic homeowner's policy, including liability. Damage to the structure is not covered under this type of policy and would be the responsibility of the property owner.

The fifth type of home policy is a complete risk policy. This type of policy covers the building and the property from any disaster that may occur.

The sixth type of home policy is condominium insurance. This policy would cover all personal property within the condo against all the disasters listed above. Liability insurance is also included. The structure and outside the condominium are the responsibility of the condominium association.

The seventh type of home policy is tailored to older homes with historic value. This policy protects against the same perils as a basic homeowner's policy but pays out actual cash value for repairs as opposed to replacement cost. Often the costs of repairing these historical homes are higher because materials used when the house was originally built are not as readily available.

As you may expect, the broader and more comprehensive the home insurance coverage, the larger the premium you can expect to pay. When considering the seven policy types, you and your agent should take the time to evaluate your personal circumstances to determine what types of coverage you need to adequately protect yourself, your family, and your home.

THE DIFFERENT PARTS OF A HOME POLICY

Now let us look at the different parts of a policy and what they cover. The first coverage part of the typical homeowner's policy insures the residence itself from damage or complete destruction caused by any of the hazards listed in the previous section. It is important to be aware, when considering this coverage type, that replacement cost and market value of your home are not the same thing. Market value is the amount of money someone would be expected to pay you to purchase your home if you were trying to sell it. This value is based on the characteristics of your home, the neighborhood you live in, and the sale price of similar homes recently sold in your area.

Replacement cost is what it would cost to completely rebuild your home from the ground up. If you do not insure your home for 100 percent of the reconstruction cost, you could be paid a depreciated amount to repair or rebuild your home. This leaves you paying the rest of the money out of pocket or sacrificing certain features you may have had in your home before the disaster struck. Your insurance agent, or insurance company representative, can help you determine replacement costs by using a computerized replacement cost calculator. Most insurance companies also require a home inspection before the policy is issued. Sometimes the home inspection can change the value from the original calculated replacement costs.

The second coverage part covers damage or destruction of detached structures. On most insurance policies, this coverage is equal to 10 percent of the total residence coverage on most insurance policies. For example, if your home is insured for $250,000, your coverage for detached structures would be $25,000. This portion of the policy covers detached garages, storage barns, and in-ground swimming pools.

It is important to remember that, if you are using your detached building or garage for any business use, the building will not be covered. If you are using the building for any business purpose, including the storage of business equipment, you should talk to your insurance agent or company representative about adding an endorsement to cover business use.

The third section of coverage insures your personal property. This includes any contents in your home not permanently attached to your dwelling, even if those items are not located in your home at the time of the loss.

If you are given the option of choosing between replacement cost and actual cash value, it is to your advantage to choose replacement cost. Replacement cost will pay the full amount to replace the stolen or damaged item, while actual cash value will pay only what your item was worth at the time of the loss.

Here is an example of how choosing replacement value coverage can be more beneficial than actual cash value coverage: Let us suppose you have a 28-inch color television that is ten years old. If you have actual cash value coverage on the contents of your home, your insurance company will base your claim payment on the amount that a ten-year-old, 28-inch color television would be worth at the time your television was stolen. A used television matching this description could be inexpensively purchased from a consignment shop, garage sale, or pawn shop, so you will not likely receive a substantial payment for your stolen television under this type of coverage. You will not be able to purchase a new television with what you would be given for your ten-year-old television.

On the other hand, if you had chosen replacement value coverage, your insurance company will pay you the amount it would cost you to purchase a new 28-inch color television with comparable features.

If you choose replacement value coverage, your insurance company will require you use the money paid on the claim to purchase replacement items. Some companies pay only the depreciated value of your items unless you show proof you replaced the item. For this reason, always keep your receipts to document the item replaced and the amount paid.

The fourth coverage portion of your home policy covers any additional living costs you may incur if your home and belongings are damaged or destroyed. The key word is additional. If you are required to find an alternate place for you and your family to live or to eat all your meals at restaurants while your home is being repaired, this coverage will pay any additional money you are paying out of your pocket monthly to live.

For example, let us suppose your home has been damaged by a fire and is unlivable while repairs are being made. Although you and your family are not able to occupy your home while workers are repairing it, you are required to make your monthly mortgage payment during this period. Your policy would pay for the cost of your temporary residence so that you would not be financially responsible for both your monthly mortgage payment and your temporary housing expenses.

The fifth coverage section is liability. This covers any property damage or injury, except damage or injury that is related to the operation, maintenance, or use of an automobile that occurs on or off your property. Examples of covered damages or injury include:

- Injuries to a child that is hurt while in your care.

- Injuries or damage that you or your child causes during a sporting event.

- Injuries that result from your dog biting a guest or passerby.

All these incidents would be covered under your home policy's liability portion. A mistake many people make is failing to understand how important this coverage is. As a result, policyholders often do not purchase high enough liability limits. Talk to your insurance agent or insurance company representative to find out how much liability coverage you should carry.

The sixth coverage section is medical payments. If a guest is injured on your property, this section can help pay for his or her medical bills. Please note that the injury does not have to be the fault of the homeowner. The accident may be a result of the guest's own misjudgment or carelessness.

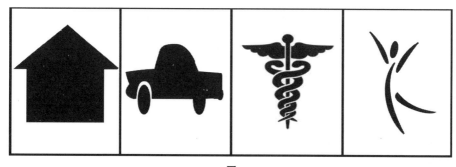

5

HOME INSURANCE DISCOUNTS & SAVINGS

This chapter is devoted to specific ways you can save money on your home insurance premiums without sacrificing the coverages you need to protect your family and satisfy your mortgage lender.

DISCOUNTS

The most important technique you can use when looking for cheap home insurance is to make sure you are taking advantage of all the possible discounts and savings available. These discounts can quickly add up, saving you hundreds of dollars or more per year. Here are some of the discounts offered on home insurance policies.

MULTILINE DISCOUNT

The multiline discount is popular among home insurance policyholders and is easy to obtain. If you already have auto coverage with a company that offers home insurance, you can save up to 15 percent on your auto insurance and home insurance premiums by placing both policies with the same insurance company or with affiliates of a single insurer. It is also to your advantage to contact other companies that offer both types of policies; have any company or agency that quotes your home insurance quote your auto as well. You may find that another company can offer you a lower rate on both policies.

SECURITY SYSTEM DISCOUNT

Most insurance companies also offer a discount if you have a security system active on your property. If your home has a security system, make sure you let your current insurance company, or any company you obtain a quote from, know this information. Also, make sure you have the paperwork available from the purchase and installation of your security system so that you can show your home insurance agent what type of system you have installed on your property. Some companies may also ask for a copy of an alarm system certificate to keep in their files. Be certain to keep your original certificate, so you can readily provide it to the insurance company.

If you do not have a security system installed, ask your insurance agent about a security system discount when you obtain your initial home insurance quote. You may be able to offset the cost of purchasing and installing a security system with your home insurance savings. Not only will you be able to continue receiving the discount on future policy terms, but you also will have the added benefit of knowing that your home, your family, and your personal property are protected from injury or loss due to vandalism, burglary, or theft.

SPRINKLER SYSTEM OR FIRE SUPPRESSANT DISCOUNT

A home insurer will frequently offer a discount if you have a sprinkler system or fire suppressant system installed in your home. As with a security system, you should have all the paperwork from the purchase and installation of your fire suppressant system available so that you can receive the discount if it is offered by your insurance company.

AGE-BASED DISCOUNT

Some companies will give discounts for people 55 and older or retired individuals. When you obtain a quote, be sure to check with your agent or insurance company to see if your company offers this discount.

PERSISTENCY DISCOUNT

Insurance companies also offer discounts for long-term customers because it costs an insurance company far less money to retain the business of current policyholders than to attract and earn the business of new policyholders. You may have to hold a policy for a few years with one company or group of insurer affiliates before you are eligible to earn this discount, but it will provide you with added savings in the long term. Because this discount can build over several policy terms, it is advantageous to find an agent and company you are happy with and keep your policy in force with the same company for as long as possible.

CLAIMS-FREE DISCOUNT

Claims-free discounts are offered by many home insurers. If you have kept your policy in force for more than one policy term and have never had a claim on a home policy, you could qualify for this discount. Ask about this discount when obtaining home insurance quotes from agents and companies to see if this discount will be available once you have completed a policy term without filing a claim.

Some insurers will allow the claims-free discount to compound over several policy terms. This means the longer you keep your home insurance policy in force without filing a claim, the greater your discount percentage will be.

To illustrate, here is an example of how a claims-free discount can benefit you in the long term:

Let us suppose your initial policy premium is $1,000 per year, and your home insurer offers a 5 percent claims-free discount for each policy term during which you keep your policy in force without filing a claim on your policy. After you complete your first policy term, you will be eligible for a 5 percent discount, so the premium for your next term will be $950.

After you have completed your second policy term without a claim, your insurer will deduct another 5 percent, so your policy premium will be 95 percent of the second term's premium, or $902.50.

If you continue your policy for another term claims-free, another 5 percent will be deducted, so your premium for the fourth term will be 95 percent of $902.50, or $857.38.

Not all home insurers that offer claims-free discounts will compound this discount, so be sure to ask your agent before you start your policy. As you can see, if your insurer allows this discount to accrue, it can add up to significant savings over several policy terms.

FIRE DEPARTMENT DISCOUNT

You can also qualify for savings on your home policy if you live close to the fire department or within city limits. Be sure to ask your agent if your insurance company offers this discount when you obtain a quote for home insurance coverage.

DEDUCTIBLES

Deductibles are another way to save a significant amount on your home insurance premiums. If you choose a low deductible on your policy, your insurer will charge a higher premium for two reasons: First, if damage or a loss occurs, your insurer will be required to make a higher payment on the claim; second, a lower deductible encourages policyholders to submit frequent, small-value claims that are costly for the insurance company to adjust and settle.

The higher the deductible you choose, the lower your premiums will be. When applying for a home insurance policy, you should choose the highest deductible you can manage without placing a strain on your family's finances. It is important you consider your deductible amount carefully because you will be responsible for that amount if you incur a loss. If the amount of damage your home or personal property incurs is less than the deductible, you will be responsible for the entire amount of the loss, regardless of whether you submit a claim to your insurance company.

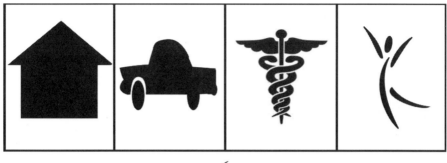

6

OBTAINING A HOME INSURANCE QUOTE

SEARCHING FOR AN AFFORDABLE QUOTE

Searching for an affordable quote can be a long and detailed process. If you do not have time to go through the phone book and call all the major home insurance companies in your area, consider going to an independent agent.

An independent agent can obtain quotes from multiple companies. This saves you time because you have to give your information only to one person, instead of multiple agents. An independent agent can also save you time by quoting you with the same coverages with each company. This saves you the time of comparing coverage amounts, deductible amounts, and endorsements line by line. You can find an independent agent by looking in the phone book.

You can also search online for an affordable home insurance quote. You can find insurance-quoting Web sites by using an online search engine or by asking friends and family if they have used any of these sites. Many of these Web sites, such as **www.homeownerswiz.com**, **www.insurance.com**, and **www.netquote.com**, offer multiple quotes and require you to enter your personal information only once.

Some of these Web sites will send your information to agents in your area who will contact you with quotes. This saves you the time of having to call multiple agents, because the agents call you. Many companies allow you to print out quotes and coverage details, so you can look them over and compare them to quotes from other companies.

HOW TO SELECT THE RIGHT QUOTE

There are many things to consider when selecting a quote. Although the lowest quote you receive will often be the most attractive, you should consider each quote carefully to make sure you are getting the best coverage at the lowest premium for you and your family.

First, make sure the company providing the quote has obtained all the necessary loss history reports and that the price is not going to change because these reports have already been factored in. If loss history reports are not considered at the time of the quote, you may end up with a higher policy premium than you expected.

Second, it is important to understand that many companies also factor credit scores and consumer reports into the quote; however, some companies do not run this information at the time of the original quote. Instead, agents can enter "good," "fair," or "poor," based on your personal assessment of your credit score and payment history when they run the quote. The agent should ask your permission to obtain your credit report and credit score before accessing your credit information from any of the three major credit-reporting agencies. If the agent does not ask your permission to obtain your credit report at the time of the quote, ask him or her if it will be obtained and if your credit score and history will be a factor in determining your eligibility for coverage or policy premiums.

Third, you should consider the replacement cost each quote is based on. If there is a significant variance in the calculated reconstruction cost on quotes from different companies, you may want to contact the agent or insurance representative to ask how the calculated reconstruction cost was determined and ask your agent why it is higher or lower than on the other quotes you receive.

Fourth, when you are selecting the right quote for you and your family, it is important to compare liability limits and deductibles between the quotes. For example, let us suppose that Company A is offering you a significantly lower premium rate than Company B. Let us also suppose that Company A is quoting you at $300,000 liability, $1,000 in medical payments, and a $1,000 deductible; Company B is quoting $500,000 liability, $3,000 in medical payments, and a $500 deductible. These quotes do not offer an accurate comparison because the liability limits and the deductibles are different. You can eliminate this issue by determining the limits you want before you start shopping for home insurance quotes and asking each agent you call or visit to quote you at your specified limits and deductible amounts.

Fifth, compare endorsements and exclusions on each policy. Each company has different guidelines regarding which endorsements are offered and which exclusions apply to a home insurance policy. What may be considered basic coverage for one company may offer you more or less coverage than basic coverage from a competing insurance company.

Most important, if you do not understand something, ask questions. Any agent or insurance representative should be willing to explain the coverages or answer any questions you have about the quote. If your agent is unwilling to answer your questions before giving you a premium quote or before submitting an application, there are many other agents and companies you can choose to help you with your home insurance needs. You do not have to receive lackluster service or inadequate explanations to obtain a home insurance policy.

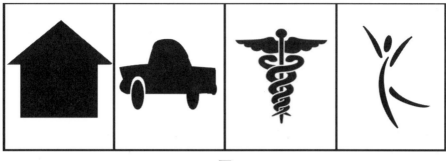

7

ADDITIONAL COVERAGES AVAILABLE ON YOUR HOME INSURANCE POLICY

In addition to the home insurance coverages described in Chapter 4, there are several endorsements that provide additional coverages. These coverages are often overlooked by insurance applicants and policyholders, but they may be necessary to protect homeowners in certain circumstances. Take a few moments to determine if these endorsements could provide valuable coverage for your home before you begin obtaining quotes and completing home insurance applications. These endorsements are worth the additional premium cost in the event of a loss and can be added to the policy for little additional premium.

BACKUP OF SEWER AND DRAINS

The backup of sewers and drains endorsement can be critical to providing adequate coverage for your home, especially if you have a finished basement. This coverage is not meant to provide coverage for weather-related floods but will cover you in the event that your drains or the sewer backs up and overflows into your home.

The specifications and requirements of this endorsement vary from company to company. It is frequently offered with either broad or limited coverage, which allows policy coverage for different types of backup and overflow scenarios. Some forms of this endorsement will not cover personal items that are damaged; however, others include personal items. Still other forms of this endorsement will cover only mechanicals that have been damaged as a result of a sewer or drain backup and overflow.

Backup of sewers and drains can cause significant damage to your home — carpet, furniture, mechanicals, and personal belongings can quickly be destroyed. Be sure to ask your agent or insurance representative to explain the types of occurrences covered by each water backup endorsement offered before deciding which one to purchase or whether to purchase this type of endorsement.

ORDINANCE OF LAW

Ordinance of law coverage pays for any upgrades that must be done to bring the home up to current building codes in the event the home must be rebuilt or repaired due to damage or loss. Without ordinance of law, your policy will pay only for repairs that are needed to pay for the loss. This leaves the policyholder left to pay the additional money to bring the home into compliance with current building codes. If the code requirements are not being met during reconstruction or repair of your home, repairs may be stopped by a building inspector. This can cause significant delays in repairing the home and can leave you with a damaged, unlivable home if you cannot pay the additional money to bring your home into compliance with local building codes.

Ordinance of law will pay for loss to any undamaged part of the home that has to be demolished to bring the rest of the home up to code, for the cost of this demolition, and for the increased reconstruction cost incurred to bring the residence into building code compliance.

Please note that if your home is less than five years old, you may want to ask your agent if you need ordinance of law coverage — the structure, mechanicals, and wiring in your home are likely new enough to be in compliance with current building standards.

Because building codes change frequently, make sure to check with your agent and your local building inspector yearly to see if any significant changes have been made. If so, it may be time to add ordinance of law coverage to your home insurance policy. This endorsement is not just for old or historical homes.

SECONDARY HOME

If you own a secondary home, do not assume that it is automatically covered under your primary home policy. Although coverage of a secondary home varies from state to state, most companies will allow you to extend your liability coverage from your primary home policy to your secondary home. However, you will need separate dwelling coverage on the secondary home in most states and with most companies. Let your agent know if you own, or are about to purchase, a secondary home. By doing so, you can ensure the home will be covered and that liability can be properly extended.

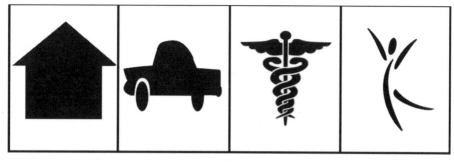

8

HOME INSURANCE & EXCLUDED NATURAL DISASTERS

Chances are you have turned on the evening news to see reports of areas destroyed by a hurricane, earthquake, or flood. Without the proper home insurance coverage, any of these disasters can destroy your home and belongings, leaving you without the resources to rebuild your home or replace your personal property. Having your home properly insured against these disasters is the easiest way to start over if one of these disasters occurs.

FLOOD

Many home insurance policyholders are not aware that flood coverage is excluded on nearly all homeowner's policies. Flood insurance must be purchased separately and carries a separate premium charge.

The National Flood Insurance Program (NFIP) is a federal program that enables you to purchase flood insurance on your home if the home is located in a designated flood zone. Although it is a federal program and is not offered by your insurance company, your agent will be able to help you secure flood insurance and can answer questions about the details of this coverage. If your home is in a flood zone, it is critical you contact your agent to inquire about securing flood coverage on your home.

A flood occurs when an excessive amount of water or mud covers land that is normally dry. A flood can occur when water rises above the normal level because of heavy rain or because of water runoff from a heavy snowfall.

Floods can also be caused by hurricanes. Although hurricane coverage is almost unheard of, a flood policy can provide coverage for water damage caused by a hurricane, while your standard home insurance policy can provide coverage for wind and projectiles.

Your choices for dealing with a flood are limited — you can be proactive and purchase flood insurance to help you recoup your loss in the event of a flood, or you can hope for assistance from the government if a flood occurs. Unfortunately, government assistance is an option only if the president declares the flood as a national disaster. Given the limited opportunity for government assistance, flood insurance is worth the investment because you have the peace of mind of knowing your home will be covered, no matter what, in the event of a flood.

When you purchase flood insurance, you can insure your home for up to $250,000 and your personal property for up to $100,000. Flood insurance is not just an option for homeowners — if you rent your home, condominium, or apartment, you can purchase coverage for your personal property for up to $100,000.

Flood insurance covers structural damage to your home; the repair or replacement of mechanicals, such as furnaces, water heaters, and air conditioners; the cleanup of debris; and the repair or replacement of flooring caused by a flood.

You can determine your flood risk and find out more about flood insurance by visiting **www.floodsmart.gov**.

EARTHQUAKE

Earthquakes are also excluded by most insurance policies. Earthquake policies are available that will cover your home in the event of a loss; however, they often carry high deductibles, which limits their effectiveness in indemnifying you for damage or a loss caused by an earthquake.

Because earthquakes are common in California, it is the state in which earthquake policies are most frequently purchased. Because of the high demand for earthquake coverage in California, the California Earthquake Authority (CEA) was developed in 2003 to provide information and advocacy for California residents seeking this coverage. If you are a California resident and are in need of earthquake insurance, you can learn more about the CEA online at **www.earthquakeauthority.com**.

Some insurance companies will also allow you to purchase an earthquake endorsement on your standard home insurance policy. In areas where earthquakes rarely occur, the endorsement will be less expensive than in areas with a higher likelihood of earthquakes.

Examine the odds of an earthquake occurring in your area when deciding if you need this endorsement or not. If you live in California or any other high-risk area, it may be worth the additional premium required to purchase this insurance. If you are not living near a fault line or an earthquake has never occurred in your area, it may not worth the extra cost to purchase earthquake insurance.

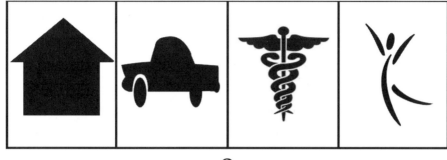

HOME INSURANCE & HOME BUSINESSES

Home businesses are often excluded from home insurance policies or have inadequate coverage to cover the risks involved with owning a home business. In this chapter, you will learn about how owning a home business affects your insurance coverage and what coverages are available for your business under your home insurance policy. You will also learn about the home business exclusions included in a typical home policy.

On a standard homeowner policy, there is no business liability. This means that, if any liability arises from your home business, no coverage for the liability will be afforded under your home insurance policy. Even if you are using a garage or detached structure on the property partially for business use, it is excluded under your policy. Coverage for any personal property for your business may be covered at low limits.

So what does that mean to a home business owner? If a client is hurt while visiting your home to discuss a business proposition or a delivery person is injured on your property while delivering a package for your business, these liabilities would be excluded. This is because, in both situations, the purpose for entering your property was business-related. This leaves you with the option of either paying out of pocket for the injury or facing a lawsuit. Injury caused to someone while you are conducting business outside the home would also be excluded.

Product liability is also excluded by the homeowner's policy. If your home business involves selling any product or service, any injury or damage caused by the product or service is excluded, leaving you open to substantial personal liability.

Worker's compensation is excluded on a home insurance policy as well. This means that, if you have employees working for or with you in your home business, there is no coverage if they are injured while assuming their job duties as your employees.

Professional liability is also excluded from home insurance policies. Professional liability covers errors made by an individual who is providing a service, such as a lawyer, accountant, insurance agent, or realtor.

There are limited business endorsements that can be added to your homeowner's policy. In many cases, these endorsements cover only businesses formed as sole proprietorships and provide a minimal amount of on-premises liability. Endorsements vary by state and by company, so check with your agent to see what business endorsements are available for your home business. If the adequate endorsements are not available, your agent can recommend a business policy that can fulfill your personal home business needs.

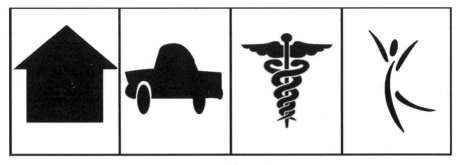

10

WHAT TO DO WHEN YOU HAVE DIFFICULTY OBTAINING HOME INSURANCE

Sometimes, it is difficult for individuals to obtain home insurance because of certain risk factors. The first step is to request quotes from insurance companies until you find a company that will insure your property. If your property has been declined by several insurance carriers, the next step is to apply to your state's assigned risk plan.

The Fair Access to Insurance Requirements (FAIR) Plan is available to provide insurance on properties considered uninsurable by most standard insurance companies. FAIR Plan policies may be more expensive than standard insurance policies and offer less coverage.

REASONS PROPERTY MAY BE DECLINED

There are several reasons a property may be declined. Homes that are in areas considered high risk for hurricanes, windstorms, tornados, and hail may be declined because there is a greater than usual risk that the home will suffer serious weather-related damages.

You may also be declined if your home has old plumbing, an outdated electrical system, or an old heating system. These homes are considered a higher risk for fire and may not meet the underwriting criteria of standard insurance companies.

If your home is in poor condition or disrepair, it may also be declined by standard insurance company guidelines. Homes are not always declined because of poor condition or lack of necessary repairs — in some cases, a company will insure the property but will provide you with a time period in which repairs must be made.

The presence of pools and trampolines may also cause you to be declined for coverage, if they are not in a fenced area. Some companies will require these items to be fenced in with a gate having a latch or lock before the property is eligible to be insured.

Even certain pets may keep you from obtaining insurance. If you own a dog considered a vicious breed by your state, you may not be eligible for insurance with your state's FAIR Plan program. Some breeds considered vicious are pit bull terriers, Rottweillers, and Presa Canarios. Check with your agent to find out more about dog breeds that may prevent you from securing home coverage.

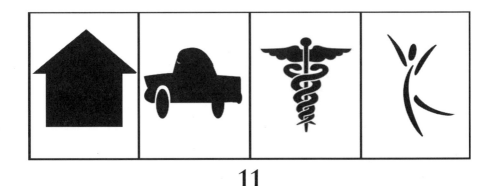

11

AUTOMOBILE INSURANCE

In the next several chapters, you will learn about how automobile insurance is designed to protect you financially, what coverages you need to adequately protect you from financial disaster, and techniques you can use to lower your automobile insurance premiums.

WHAT IS AUTOMOBILE INSURANCE?

Owning and operating an automobile is a necessity for most people today. Unless you live in a large, compact city with a sophisticated public transportation system, you need an automobile to go to work, run errands, and visit friends and family.

Although owning and operating a motor vehicle is often a necessity rather than a luxury, having an automobile drastically increases the amount of personal risk you assume on a daily basis. Every time you get behind the wheel of an automobile, you are placing yourself and the other occupants of the vehicle at risk of physical injury or even death. You also run the risk of damaging or destroying your motor vehicle in an accident or causing damage to another motor vehicle or the personal property of another person.

Even when your automobile is parked, owning a motor vehicle still increases your financial risk. Your motor vehicle could be damaged or destroyed by a wide range of hazards, such as falling trees, theft, vandalism, or severe weather, such as wind, hail, or falling ice. If you park your automobile on the street, your motor vehicle is also at risk of being struck by another vehicle.

Automobile insurance is designed to financially protect you against losses that may result from these kinds of risks. A typical automobile insurance policy contains several coverages, each of which protect you against a specific type of financial loss.

Depending on the types of coverages you choose, automobile insurance can pay for injury or death you cause to others as a result of an accident for which you are cited by the police or otherwise found at fault; for property damage you cause to the motor vehicles or possessions of others; for injury or property damage you sustain as a result of an accident or loss; and some of the incidental expenses you may be responsible for after a loss.

You should choose the coverages that best fit your financial needs based on a variety of factors, including the value of your vehicle, other insurance you may already carry, and the savings or other financial reserves you have available to pay for expenses resulting from a motor vehicle accident or loss.

WHY DO YOU NEED AFFORDABLE AUTOMOBILE INSURANCE?

Few people would disagree that owning, operating, and maintaining a motor vehicle is an expensive proposition. Simply purchasing a reliable motor vehicle is expensive — even the economy cars offered by major automobile manufacturers are becoming as expensive as the near-luxury cars of a decade ago. If you have a family and need a full-sized sedan, you can expect to pay more than $20,000 for a new model. This can take $400 to $500 out of your budget each month, before the other expenses of owning a motor vehicle are considered.

Once you have purchased an automobile, there are a variety of other expenses that can further deplete your budget. Routine maintenance, such as oil changes, tire rotations, and transmission flushes are required to ensure the continued reliability and safety of your automobile. Add gasoline costs, registration, and inspection fees, and you can easily spend another $200 to $300 per month just to drive your motor vehicle.

It is little wonder most people wince when they see the amount automobile insurance will add to their household expenses. In the United States, drivers pay an average of about $815 yearly for automobile insurance. In the most expensive states for automobile insurance, New York and New Jersey, drivers pay an average annual premium of more than $1,100; in the least expensive states, Maine and Iowa, drivers still pay about $600 yearly.

Although it represents a significant expense for motorists, automobile insurance is required under the laws of many states. Failure to purchase and maintain at least the minimum amount of automobile insurance required by the state you live in can result in fines, impoundment of your vehicle, or even time in prison.

Mandatory state insurance requirements aside, automobile insurance is a necessity because of the risk of substantial financial loss you face when you own and operate a vehicle. A single accident can cost you hundreds of thousands of dollars in legal liabilities for damage or injury to others and medical expenses or property damage sustained by you or your family.

Since automobile insurance is a necessity that helps you and your family prevent financial disaster, it is important that you budget for automobile insurance premiums along with your other expenses. It is also important that you take advantage of every opportunity available to reduce your premiums without reducing your needed coverages.

Knowing the types of coverages available and how they can help you protect your family's finances is the first step toward obtaining the automobile insurance you need at a price that you can live with.

TYPES OF AUTOMOBILE INSURANCE

To help you better understand what automobile insurance does and help you decide which coverages you need, this section will describe the types of coverages offered under an automobile insurance policy so that in the Chapter 13 you can understand the types of policy packages an insurance agent or company is likely to offer you.

Types of Coverage
Bodily Injury Liability Coverage

If you are found at fault for an accident with another vehicle or if you strike a pedestrian with your automobile, you will be held liable for the physical injuries caused to other people in your own vehicle, occupants of another vehicle involved in the accident, and pedestrians stuck by your vehicle or injured while avoiding being struck by your vehicle.

Bodily injury liability coverage pays for the injuries you cause while operating a motor vehicle, up to the policy limits you select when you purchase your automobile insurance policy.

You should select your bodily injury liability limits based on the maximum amount of injury you or your agent think could be caused by a single accident and the net worth of your personal assets that would be at risk if you did not have bodily injury liability coverage in place. Policy limits for bodily injury liability coverage can be expressed as either a split limit or a combined single limit.

A split limit means the insurance policy provides one maximum payment for bodily injury to one person and a higher limit for bodily injury to two or more people. For example, let us suppose you purchase a split bodily injury liability coverage limit of $100,000/$300,000. Here are the maximum amounts your policy would pay for bodily injury you cause to others in several scenarios:

- If you cause an accident in which Joe Smith was the sole occupant of the vehicle and Joe sustained $80,000 in physical injuries, your policy would pay Joe $80,000.

- If you cause an accident in which Joe Smith was the sole occupant of the vehicle and Joe sustained $120,000 in physical injuries, your policy would pay Joe $100,000 because $100,000 is your bodily injury liability coverage limit per person. You would be responsible for the additional $20,000 of Joe's injuries.

- If you cause an accident in which Joe and Jan Smith were the only occupants of the other vehicle and both Joe and Jan sustained $120,000 in physical injuries each, your policy would pay Joe and

Jan a total of $200,000 because payment for each person's injuries is capped at $100,000. You would be responsible for the remaining $40,000.

- If you cause an accident in which Joe, Jan, Jerry, and Jim Smith sustain $50,000 in physical injuries each, your policy would pay each injured person $50,000 for a total of $200,000 because each person's injuries are within the $100,000 per person limit and the total of all the injuries is within the $300,000 policy limit.

- If you cause an accident in which Joe, Jan, Jerry, and Jim Smith sustain $100,000 in physical injuries each, your policy would pay each injured person $75,000 because your policy has a total bodily policy limit of $300,000, regardless of how many people are injured. You would be responsible for the remaining $100,000.

A combined single limit means payment for injuries is subject to a single policy limit per accident, regardless of how many people are injured. For example, if you purchased a policy with a combined single limit of $300,000 and you caused an accident in which a single driver sustained $200,000 in injuries, your policy would pay the entire amount of that driver's injury expenses. If you caused an accident in which four people sustained $100,000 in injuries each, your policy would pay each injured person $75,000 because the total of all drivers' injuries would exceed the combined single limit of $300,000. You would pay the remaining $100,000.

Property Damage Liability Coverage

Like bodily injury liability coverage, property damage liability coverage protects your financial assets if you are found at fault in an automobile accident. This coverage pays for the damage you cause to another vehicle in an accident. It also pays for damage to the personal property of others that results from an accident you cause. This includes damage to personal property being transported in another motor vehicle involved in an accident; fixtures such as light poles, utility poles, or fences; and homes and other buildings.

Property damage liability is expressed as a single limit, which represents the highest amount that your insurance company will pay for property damage resulting from a single accident. This limit does not change regardless of how many people's property you damage or how much total property damage you cause.

As with bodily injury liability coverage, you should select your policy limit based on the amount of financial assets you and your agent believe are at risk and the maximum amount of property damage you believe you could cause if you were at fault in an automobile accident. It is important not to underestimate this amount, because you will be legally liable for any damages in excess of your property damage policy limit.

Medical Payments Coverage

Many companies offer medical payments coverage as a part of their automobile insurance policies. This coverage pays for medical expenses you or the occupants of your vehicle sustain as a result of a motor vehicle accident, regardless of who is at fault. Medical payments coverage is offered at limits that are substantially lower than your bodily injury liability and property damage liability limits.

Medical payments coverage is not meant to replace health insurance coverage but rather to pay for medical expenses not covered by your health insurance for a variety of reasons. This can include amounts not payable by health insurance because of deductibles or coinsurance requirements or because of health insurance policy limits.

For this reason, some companies label this coverage Excess Medical Payments to emphasize the fact that any available health insurance must pay for your injuries and those of the other occupants of your vehicle before this coverage will pay under your automobile insurance policy.

Personal Injury Protection Coverage

Personal injury protection coverage is available only in a small number of states. Elements of this coverage are mandated by states in which this coverage is available.

The elements of personal injury protection coverage are designed to cover expenses other than property damage expenses, that you or an additional insured sustain as a result of a motor vehicle accident. This coverage is not available to occupants of your vehicle that are not listed as additional insureds on the declarations page of your policy.

Personal injury protection is considered no-fault coverage, which means each person's insurance company is responsible for that person's injuries. Legislatures of states that require insurers to offer personal injury protection believe a no-fault system reduces the number of lawsuits brought against other motorists.

Here are the personal injury protection coverages that may be offered by insurance companies under your state's insurance laws. The specific coverages vary by state, and your state may require insurance companies to offer some, all, or none of these coverages:

- **Medical expenses.** This element of personal injury protection coverage is similar to the medical payments coverage described previously, but it does not necessarily require health insurance to pay for your medical expenses before this coverage can be used.

- **Rehabilitation expenses.** This element pays for expenses for rehabilitative services you or an additional insured require while recovering from injuries sustained in a motor vehicle accident. This can include physical therapy or other services designed to help you return to mobility and employment.

- **In-home service expenses.** Care services that require a healthcare professional to come to your home to perform the services are covered under this element of personal injury protection coverage. This coverage is valuable if your injuries confine you to your home for an extended time but you still require ongoing medical care.

In-home services coverage may also pay for a variety of nonmedical services. In some states, these can include hiring professionals to get your groceries, clean your home, or even mow your lawn. States that require insurers to offer this coverage set a maximum amount of coverage per day and a time limit beyond which insurance companies are not required to make continued payments.

- **Disability income loss.** This element pays for a portion of your lost wages if you are unable to work because of injuries sustained in a motor vehicle accident. Each state that requires this coverage sets a time limit and a maximum monthly amount for payments made to you under this coverage.

- **Funeral and burial expenses.** If you are killed in a motor vehicle accident, the funeral and burial expenses element of personal injury protection coverage will pay a set amount for your funeral and for the cost of your burial or cremation.

- **Extraordinary medical benefits.** This element pays for high medical expenses that exhaust your medical expenses or health insurance coverage. This element is inexpensive to purchase because of the low likelihood your injuries will be severe enough to trigger payment under this coverage.

- **Survivor benefits.** This element of personal injury protection coverage pays your survivors if you are killed in a motor vehicle accident. Payments may include a portion of the wages you would have earned if the accident would not have occurred or continued medical or nonmedical in-home services.

Uninsured Motorist Bodily Injury Coverage

Although the laws of many states require all drivers to carry automobile insurance, some drivers choose not to purchase insurance for their vehicles. If you are struck by an uninsured driver, either as an occupant of a vehicle or as a pedestrian, you will be responsible for paying for your own medical expenses unless you have purchased uninsured motorist bodily injury coverage.

Uninsured motorist bodily injury coverage pays for physical injuries that you or the other occupants of your vehicle sustain as a result of a motor vehicle accident caused by an uninsured driver. It also pays for injury to you or an additional insured on your policy if you are struck by an uninsured motorist while not occupying a vehicle.

Like bodily injury liability coverage, uninsured motorist bodily injury is sold as either a split limit or a combined single limit coverage. Split limit coverage provides a maximum per person limit for bodily injury to one person and a higher per policy limit for accidents where two or more people are injured as a result of an uninsured driver's actions. Combined single limit coverage provides a per accident limit, regardless of how many people are injured. You can purchase uninsured motorist bodily injury coverage limits up to or equal to your bodily injury liability limits.

When your insurance company pays you under your uninsured motorist coverage, it reserves the right to attempt to collect amounts it has paid to you from the uninsured driver. This right is called the right to subrogation. This means that, once your insurance company has paid you for your injuries, you will no longer have the legal right to seek payment from the driver who caused the accident.

Different states have varying laws regarding accidents in which the driver at fault cannot be identified, such as a driver who left the scene of the accident before police arrived. Most will allow you to recover under your uninsured motorist coverage if you can provide evidence that another driver caused the accident, such as testimony from another vehicle occupant or a third party that was not involved in the accident. Some states do not allow insurance companies to require evidence before providing payment for an accident under your uninsured motorist bodily injury coverage.

Underinsured Motorist Bodily Injury Coverage

If you carry high bodily injury liability coverage limits and you are struck by a motorist that carries lower liability limits, the other driver's insurance company will not pay for any injuries above the other driver's bodily injury liability limits. This creates a situation in which you are providing more protection for other drivers on the road than you are being provided by the driver who caused the accident.

Some states require insurers to also offer underinsured motorist bodily injury coverage, which pays for bodily injury amounts above the other driver's liability limits. You can purchase underinsured motorist bodily injury coverage with limits up to or equal to your bodily injury liability limits. Like bodily injury liability, underinsured motorist bodily injury coverage can be purchased with either a split limit or a combined single limit.

To give an example of how underinsured motorist bodily injury coverage works, let us suppose you carry bodily injury liability limits of $100,000 per person and $300,000 per accident. Suppose you are in an accident for which the other driver is at fault, and you sustain $100,000 in injuries as a result of the accident. When you contact the other driver's insurance company, you learn the driver carries bodily injury liability limits of $25,000 per person and $50,000 per accident.

The other driver's insurance company will pay you $25,000 for your injuries because that is the maximum amount payable per person under that driver's policy. If you have purchased underinsured motorist bodily injury coverage with limits equal to your bodily injury liability limits, your policy will pay you $75,000.

Now, let us suppose the same driver causes an accident in which you and another occupant of the vehicle each sustain injuries of $150,000 each. The other driver's policy would pay you $50,000 for injuries, and your underinsured motorist coverage would pay $150,000 of the remaining amount for injuries because of the $100,000 per-person cap on this coverage.

Uninsured motorist bodily injury and underinsured motorist bodily injury are sometimes sold as a single coverage, which simply means that your insurance company will charge one premium for the two coverages, instead of charging for the coverages separately. Each state's insurance laws dictate whether uninsured motorist bodily injury and underinsured motorist bodily injury are available as a single coverage or separate coverages.

Uninsured Motorist Property Damage

Some states require insurance companies to offer uninsured motorist property damage coverage to automobile insurance applicants. Uninsured motorist property damage pays for damage to your vehicle or personal property that results from an accident caused by an uninsured motorist. If your insurance company offers this coverage, you can purchase uninsured motorist property damage coverage with a limit of up to or equal to your property damage liability limit.

As with uninsured motorist bodily injury coverage, when you accept a payment under uninsured motorist property damage coverage, you may give up the right to pursue payment from the driver who caused the accident.

Comprehensive Coverage (Also Other than Collision Coverage)

Comprehensive coverage pays for damages to your motor vehicle that happen as a result of an occurrence other than a motor vehicle accident with another vehicle or a single-car accident in which your vehicle collides with a stationary object, such as a tree, a building, or the ground.

The following occurrences are examples of comprehensive losses:

- Your vehicle collides with an animal, such as a deer, bear, or cow.

- Your vehicle is struck by a bird, gravel, or other airborne object.

- Damage to your vehicle is caused by fire that originates from within the automobile, such as in the engine.

- Your vehicle is vandalized while parked on the street.

- Someone other than a resident of your household steals your vehicle, and it cannot be recovered.

- A tree falls on your parked vehicle.

Payment for a comprehensive loss to your motor vehicle is payable in one of two ways:

- If the amount of comprehensive damage to your vehicle is less than the actual cash value of your vehicle at the time of the loss, your policy will pay the amount required to repair the vehicle.

- If the amount of the comprehensive damage to your vehicle is greater than the actual cash value of your vehicle at the time of the loss, your policy will pay the actual cash value of the vehicle.

Because the likelihood of a comprehensive loss to your motor vehicle is significantly lower than the likelihood of collision damage, comprehensive premiums are lower than collision premiums.

Collision Coverage

Collision coverage pays for damage to your motor vehicle that is caused by a collision with another vehicle or a collision of your vehicle with a stationary object.

The following occurrences are examples of collision losses:

- While driving your motor vehicle, your vehicle travels left of center on a two-lane road and strikes another vehicle.

- While driving your motor vehicle, your vehicle slides off the shoulder of the road and collides with a tree.

- While traveling on a freeway, the traffic in front of you suddenly comes to a halt, and you collide with the vehicle in front of you.

Like comprehensive coverage, collision coverage pays the lower amount, whether it is the damage or the actual cash value of the vehicle at the time of the loss. When you are involved in an accident that is classified as a collision, collision coverage pays for damage to your vehicle regardless of who was at fault in the accident.

There are certain circumstances under which payment may be denied for collision coverage. For instance, if you were engaging in an illegal activity at the time of the accident, such as fleeing a law enforcement officer or transporting controlled substances, your insurance policy may not extend coverage for damage to your motor vehicle.

Rental Coverage

Some insurance policies also offer coverage that pays for you to rent a vehicle if your own motor vehicle is damaged or destroyed in an accident. This is offered as an optional coverage.

Rental coverage pays a specified amount per day for vehicle rental and is limited to a specific number of days or until your damaged vehicle has been repaired or replaced, whichever comes first.

Towing and Roadside Coverage

Another optional coverage offered by many automobile insurance companies is towing and roadside coverage. The specifics of this coverage vary from company to company — some may pay for towing only if your vehicle is in an accident; others pay for towing for accidents and mechanical breakdowns; and still others pay for additional services, such as tire changes, winching, and gasoline delivery.

Insurers that offer towing and roadside coverage place restrictions on how much they will pay for towing and other services and limit the number of times you can make claims under this coverage during a given policy period.

If you do not subscribe to a roadside assistance service, such as the American Automobile Association (AAA), this can be a valuable coverage to add to your policy. The premiums for this coverage are quite reasonable, and the coverage can be valuable if you become stranded while driving.

Gap Insurance

With the cost of cars rising, many people have no choice but to take out a lease or loan on a vehicle because they do not have the funds available to buy the car outright. To keep payments lower, many auto finance companies and banks have begun to offer longer-term loans. It is not unusual to have a five- to six-year loan if you purchase a brand-new or newer used vehicle.

What many people do not realize is the value of your car depreciates, or decreases, almost as soon as you drive the car off the lot. This is true for brand-new vehicles that can decrease in value by thousands of dollars before you park in your driveway for the first time.

Now you are left with a vehicle that you paid $20,000 for but that is worth only $17,000 by the time you get it home. But this does not change the fact that you are left paying off your $20,000 loan. You are responsible for the balance of this loan no matter what happens.

Now, let us say about a week after you buy the vehicle, you are traveling and lose control of the vehicle and go off the road. You are all right, but you have managed to do enough damage to your vehicle for an insurance adjuster to rule it a total loss.

You have insurance, so the loan with your bank or finance company will be paid off and you will simply go purchase a new car, right? Wrong. Your insurance company will pay you only the depreciated value of the vehicle, leaving you responsible for paying the thousands of dollars left over with your loan company.

Now, not only are you going to have to finance another vehicle, but you are going to be left paying the remainder of a loan for a vehicle you do not have anymore — unless you have purchased gap insurance.

Just as the word "gap" indicates, gap insurance will pay the difference between the depreciated value your insurance company pays and the loan balance. This will leave you completely free from the loan on your totaled vehicle and able to start fresh with a new vehicle.

Gap insurance is normally not costly and can be built into your car payments if purchased when you buy the car. Many dealerships will offer gap insurance when you are signing the paperwork on your new vehicle. Gap insurance policies normally range anywhere from $250 to $500, and the coverage lasts for the life of the loan. This is an extra expense, but it is well worth it.

It is always a good idea to check with your insurance agent about gap insurance before purchasing a new vehicle. It does not take long to quote, and many times your insurance agent can offer you a lower rate than you will be offered by a car dealership. The only possible disadvantage to purchasing gap from your agent is you will not be able to have it built into your loan payment, unless you are with an insurance company that also offers vehicle loans. Another possible disadvantage is some gap insurance companies require your agent to collect the entire fee for the policy up front.

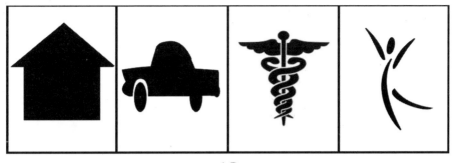

12

STATE AUTOMOBILE INSURANCE REQUIREMENTS

This chapter will list the coverages auto insurance companies must offer in each state. It will also list the coverages that are mandatory in each state and the ones you may reject, either verbally or in writing.

ALABAMA

Minimum liability limits: $20,000 per person, $40,000 per accident for bodily injury liability, $10,000 per accident for property damage liability. You may also purchase a $50,000 bond or place $50,000 on deposit with the Division of Motor Vehicles in lieu of purchasing an insurance policy. If you own more than 25 vehicles, you may claim a self-insurance exemption from the insurance, bond, or deposit requirement. Alabama is not a no-fault state and does not allow insurers to offer personal injury protection coverage.

Minimum uninsured motorist limits: $20,000 per person, $40,000 per accident for bodily injury. Uninsured motorist bodily injury coverage includes underinsured motorist bodily injury coverage. You may reject this coverage either verbally or in writing. There are no stated minimum requirements for uninsured motorist property damage coverage — your insurance company is not required to offer this coverage to you.

ALASKA

Minimum liability limits: $50,000 per person, $100,000 per accident for bodily injury liability, $25,000 per accident for property damage liability. Alaska allows self-insurance for fleet vehicles. Alaska is not a no-fault state and does not allow insurers to offer personal injury protection coverage.

Minimum uninsured motorist limits: $50,000 per person, $100,000 per accident for bodily injury, $25,000 for uninsured motorist property damage. Uninsured motorist bodily injury coverage includes underinsured motorist bodily injury coverage. You may reject uninsured motorist bodily injury and uninsured motorist property damage in writing.

ARIZONA

Minimum liability limits: $15,000 per person, $30,000 per accident for bodily injury liability, $10,000 per accident for property damage liability. You may also purchase a bond or place $40,000 on deposit with the Division of Motor Vehicles in lieu of purchasing an insurance policy. If you own more than 25 vehicles, you may claim a self-insurance exemption from the insurance, bond, or deposit requirement. Arizona is not a no-fault state and does not allow insurers to offer personal injury protection coverage.

Minimum uninsured motorist limits: $15,000 per person, $30,000 per

accident for bodily injury. You may reject this coverage in writing. There are no stated minimum requirements for uninsured motorist property damage coverage — your insurance company is not required to offer this coverage to you. Minimum underinsured motorist limits: $15,000 per person, $30,000 per accident for bodily injury. You may reject this coverage in writing.

ARKANSAS

Minimum liability limits: $25,000 per person, $50,000 per accident for bodily injury liability, $25,000 per accident for property damage liability. You may also purchase a bond or place $75,000 on deposit with the Division of Motor Vehicles in lieu of purchasing an insurance policy. If you own more than 25 vehicles, you may claim a self-insurance exemption from the insurance, bond, or deposit requirement.

Minimum personal injury protection coverage: $5,000 per person for medical and hospital expenses; 70 percent of lost wages, up to $140 per week for 52 weeks; $5,000 for accidental death; $70 per week for replacement services.

Minimum uninsured motorist limits: $25,000 per person, $50,000 per accident for bodily injury, $25,000 per accident for uninsured motorist property damage. You may reject this coverage in writing. Minimum underinsured motorist limits: $25,000 per person, $50,000 per accident for bodily injury. You may reject this coverage in writing.

CALIFORNIA

Minimum liability limits: $15,000 per person, $30,000 per accident for bodily injury liability, $5,000 per accident for property damage liability. If you meet certain income restrictions, you may also qualify for a low cost policy with limits of $10,000 per person and $20,000 per accident for bodily injury liability and $3,000 for property damage liability. You may also purchase a bond or place a deposit with the Department of Motor Vehicles for an amount determined by the Department, in lieu of purchasing an insurance policy. If you own more than 25 vehicles, you may claim a self-insurance exemption from the insurance, bond, or deposit requirement. California is not a no-fault state and does not allow insurers to offer personal injury protection coverage.

Minimum uninsured motorist limits: $15,000 per person, $30,000 per accident for bodily injury, actual cash value or $3,500 (whichever is less) for uninsured motorist property damage. Uninsured motorist bodily injury coverage includes underinsured motorist bodily injury coverage. You may reject uninsured motorist bodily coverage in writing and uninsured motorist property damage either verbally or in writing.

COLORADO

Minimum liability limits: $25,000 per person, $50,000 per accident for bodily injury liability, $15,000 per accident for property damage liability. You may also purchase a bond or place $35,000 on deposit with the Division of Motor Vehicles in lieu of purchasing an insurance policy. If you own more than 25 vehicles, you may claim a self-insurance exemption from the insurance, bond, or deposit requirement. Colorado is not a no-fault state and does not allow insurers to offer personal injury protection coverage.

Minimum uninsured motorist limits: $25,000 per person, $50,000 per accident for bodily injury, actual cash value or the cost of repairs (whichever is less) for uninsured motorist property damage. Uninsured motorist bodily injury coverage includes underinsured motorist bodily injury coverage. You may reject uninsured motorist bodily injury coverage in writing. Uninsured motorist property damage coverage is optional and does not require a verbal or written rejection.

CONNECTICUT

Minimum liability limits: $20,000 per person, $40,000 per accident for bodily injury liability, $10,000 per accident for property damage liability. You may also purchase a bond or place a deposit with the Division of Motor Vehicles in lieu of purchasing an insurance policy. If you own more than 25 vehicles, you may claim a self-insurance exemption from the insurance, bond, or deposit requirement. Connecticut is not a no-fault state and does not allow insurers to offer personal injury protection coverage.

Minimum uninsured motorist limits: $20,000 per person, $40,000 per accident for bodily injury. Uninsured motorist bodily injury coverage includes underinsured motorist bodily injury coverage. You may reject this coverage in writing. There are no stated minimum requirements for uninsured motorist property damage coverage — your insurance company is not required to offer this coverage to you.

DELAWARE

Minimum liability limits: $15,000 per person, $30,000 per accident for bodily injury liability, $10,000 per accident for property damage liability. You may also purchase a $30,000 bond or place $30,000 on deposit with the Division of Motor Vehicles in lieu of purchasing an insurance policy. If you own more than 15 vehicles, you may claim a self-insurance exemption from the insurance, bond, or deposit requirement.

Minimum personal injury protection coverage: $15,000 per person, $30,000 per accident for medical and hospital expenses, loss of earnings, replacement services, and survivorship benefits; $5,000 for funeral expenses.

Minimum uninsured motorist limits: $15,000 per person, $30,000 per

accident for bodily injury, $10,000 per accident for uninsured motorist property damage. Uninsured motorist bodily injury coverage includes underinsured motorist bodily injury coverage. You may reject this coverage in writing.

DISTRICT OF COLUMBIA

Minimum liability limits: $15,000 per person, $30,000 per accident for bodily injury liability, $10,000 per accident for property damage liability. If you own more than 25 vehicles, you may claim a self-insurance exemption from the insurance, bond, or deposit requirement.

Minimum personal injury protection coverage: $50,000 for medical and rehabilitation expenses; $12,000 for loss of income, less 20 percent for taxes; all reasonable replacement services for three years; $4,000 for funeral expenses.

Minimum uninsured motorist limits: $25,000 per person, $50,000 per accident for bodily injury, $5,000 for uninsured motorist property damage. You may not reject uninsured motorist bodily injury or uninsured motorist property damage coverage. Minimum underinsured motorist limits: $25,000 per person, $50,000 per accident for bodily injury. You may reject this coverage either verbally or in writing.

FLORIDA

Minimum liability limits: Florida does not have a minimum requirement for bodily injury liability but requires drivers to purchase a policy with limits of at least $10,000 per accident for property damage liability or $30,000 combined bodily injury liability and property damage liability.

Minimum personal injury protection coverage: $10,000 for medical expenses and survivorship benefits.

Minimum uninsured motorist limits: $10,000 per person, $30,000 per accident for bodily injury. Uninsured motorist bodily injury coverage includes underinsured motorist bodily injury coverage. You may reject this coverage in writing. There are no stated minimum requirements for uninsured motorist property damage coverage — your insurance company is not required to offer this coverage to you.

GEORGIA

Minimum liability limits: $25,000 per person, $50,000 per accident for bodily injury liability, $25,000 per accident for property damage liability. You may also purchase a bond or place a deposit with the Division of Motor Vehicles in lieu of purchasing an insurance policy. If you own a large number of vehicles, you may claim a self-insurance exemption from the insurance, bond, or deposit requirement. Georgia is not a no-fault state and does not allow insurers to offer personal injury protection coverage.

Minimum uninsured motorist limits: $25,000 per person, $50,000 per accident for bodily injury, $25,000 for uninsured motorist property damage. Uninsured motorist bodily injury coverage includes underinsured motorist bodily injury coverage. You may reject this coverage in writing.

HAWAII

Minimum liability limits: $20,000 per person, $40,000 per accident for bodily injury liability, $10,000 per accident for property damage liability. If you own more than 25 vehicles, you may claim a self-insurance exemption from the insurance, bond, or deposit requirement.

Minimum personal injury protection coverage: $10,000 per person for all personal injury protection coverages.

Minimum uninsured motorist limits: $20,000 per person, $40,000 per accident for bodily injury, $10,000 for uninsured motorist property damage. You may reject this coverage in writing. Minimum underinsured motorist limits: $20,000 per person, $40,000 per accident for bodily injury. You may reject this coverage either verbally or in writing.

IDAHO

Minimum liability limits: $25,000 per person, $50,000 per accident for bodily injury liability, $5,000 per accident for property damage liability. You may also purchase a $50,000 bond in lieu of purchasing an insurance policy. If you own more than 25 vehicles, you may claim a self-insurance exemption from the insurance, bond, or deposit requirement. Idaho is not a no-fault state and does not allow insurers to offer personal injury protection coverage.

Minimum uninsured motorist limits: $25,000 per person, $50,000 per accident for bodily injury. You may reject this coverage in writing. There are no stated minimum requirements for uninsured motorist property damage coverage — your insurance company is not required to offer this coverage to you. Minimum underinsured motorist limits: Underinsured motorist bodily injury is an optional coverage. There are no stated minimum limits, and a rejection is not required.

ILLINOIS

Minimum liability limits: $20,000 per person, $40,000 per accident for bodily injury liability, $15,000 per accident for property damage liability. You may also purchase a bond or place a deposit with the Division of Motor

Vehicles in lieu of purchasing an insurance policy. If you own more than 25 vehicles, you may claim a self-insurance exemption from the insurance, bond, or deposit requirement. Illinois is not a no-fault state and does not allow insurers to offer personal injury protection coverage.

Minimum uninsured motorist limits: $20,000 per person, $40,000 per accident for bodily injury, $15,000 or the actual cash value of the vehicle for uninsured motorist property damage. You may not reject uninsured motorist bodily injury coverage; however, you may reject uninsured motorist property damage coverage either verbally or in writing. Minimum underinsured motorist limits: $20,000 per person, $40,000 per accident for bodily injury. You may not reject underinsured motorist bodily injury coverage.

INDIANA

Minimum liability limits: $25,000 per person, $50,000 per accident for bodily injury liability, $10,000 per accident for property damage liability. You may also place $40,000 on deposit with the Division of Motor Vehicles in lieu of purchasing an insurance policy. If you own a large number of vehicles, you may claim a self-insurance exemption from the insurance, bond, or deposit requirement. Indiana is not a no-fault state and does not allow insurers to offer personal injury protection coverage.

Minimum uninsured motorist limits: $25,000 per person, $50,000 per accident for bodily injury, $10,000 for uninsured motorist property damage. You may reject this coverage in writing. Minimum underinsured motorist limits: $25,000 per person, $50,000 per accident for underinsured motorist bodily injury coverage. You may reject this coverage in writing.

IOWA

Minimum liability limits: $20,000 per person, $40,000 per accident for bodily injury liability, $15,000 per accident for property damage liability. You may also purchase a $55,000 bond or place $55,000 on deposit with the Division of Motor Vehicles in lieu of purchasing an insurance policy. If you own more than 25 vehicles, you may claim a self-insurance exemption from the insurance, bond, or deposit requirement. Iowa is not a no-fault state and does not allow insurers to offer personal injury protection coverage.

Minimum uninsured motorist limits: $20,000 per person, $40,000 per accident for bodily injury. You may reject this coverage in writing. There are no stated minimum requirements for uninsured motorist property damage coverage — your insurance company is not required to offer this coverage to you. Minimum underinsured motorist limits: $20,000 per person, $40,000 per accident for underinsured motorist bodily injury. You may reject this coverage in writing.

KANSAS

Minimum liability limits: $25,000 per person, $50,000 per accident for bodily injury liability, $10,000 per accident for property damage liability. If you own more than 25 vehicles, you may claim a self-insurance exemption from the insurance, bond, or deposit requirement.

Minimum personal injury protection coverage: $4,500 for medical expenses; $4,500 for rehabilitation expenses; 85 percent of lost wages, up to $900 per month for one year; $25 per day for replacement services for one year; survivorship benefits equal to lost wages and rehabilitation limits; $2,000 per person for funeral expenses.

Minimum uninsured motorist limits: $20,000 per person, $40,000 per accident for bodily injury. You may reject only the portion of this coverage that exceeds your bodily injury liability and property damage liability limits. The rejection of these excess limits must be made in writing. There are no stated minimum requirements for uninsured motorist property damage coverage — your insurance company is not required to offer this coverage to you.

KENTUCKY

Minimum liability limits: $20,000 per person, $40,000 per accident for bodily injury liability, $15,000 per accident for property damage liability. You may elect to purchase a combined limit policy with a minimum limit of $60,000 for bodily injury liability and property damage liability. You may also purchase a $55,000 bond or place $55,000 on deposit with the Division of Motor Vehicles in lieu of purchasing an insurance policy. If you own more than 25 vehicles, you may claim a self-insurance exemption from the insurance, bond, or deposit requirement.

Minimum personal injury protection coverage: $1,000 per person for medical expenses; $200 per week for lost wages; $200 per week for replacement services; $200 per week for survivor benefits; $1,000 for funeral expenses. The total of all benefits under this coverage is subject to a $10,000 maximum if minimum limits are purchased.

Minimum uninsured motorist limits: $20,000 per person, $40,000 per accident for bodily injury. You may reject this coverage in writing. There are no stated minimum requirements for uninsured motorist property damage coverage — your insurance company is not required to offer this coverage to you. Minimum underinsured motorist limits: $20,000 per person, $40,000 per accident for underinsured motorist bodily injury. You may reject this coverage in writing.

LOUISIANA

Minimum liability limits: $10,000 per person, $20,000 per accident for bodily injury liability, $10,000 per accident for property damage liability. You may also purchase a bond or place $30,000 on deposit with the Division of Motor Vehicles in lieu of purchasing an insurance policy. If you own more than 25 vehicles or have $100,000 available for property damage liability, you may claim a self-insurance exemption from the insurance, bond, or deposit requirement. Louisiana is not a no-fault state and does not allow insurers to offer personal injury protection coverage.

Minimum uninsured motorist limits: $10,000 per person, $20,000 per accident for bodily injury, $10,000 or the actual cash value of the vehicle for uninsured motorist property damage. Uninsured motorist bodily injury coverage includes underinsured motorist bodily injury coverage. You may reject this coverage in writing or select economic benefits only.

MAINE

Minimum liability limits: $50,000 per person, $100,000 per accident for bodily injury liability, $25,000 per accident for property damage liability. You may also place a deposit equal to the minimum policy limits with the Division of Motor Vehicles in lieu of purchasing an insurance policy. Medical payments limits: $1,000 per person. Maine is not a no-fault state and does not allow insurers to offer personal injury protection coverage.

Minimum uninsured motorist limits: $50,000 per person, $100,000 per accident for bodily injury. Uninsured motorist bodily injury coverage includes underinsured motorist bodily injury coverage. You may not reject this coverage.

MARYLAND

Minimum liability limits: $20,000 per person, $40,000 per accident for bodily injury liability, $15,000 per accident for property damage liability. You may also use other forms of financial responsibility approved by the Motor Vehicle Administration in lieu of purchasing an insurance policy. In certain circumstances, you may claim a self-insurance exemption from the insurance requirement.

Minimum personal injury protection coverage: $2,500 for medical expenses, 85 percent of lost wages for up to three years, reasonable replacement services for three years. The total of all coverages is subject to a $2,500 maximum when personal injury protection coverage is purchased at the minimum limits.

Minimum uninsured motorist limits: $20,000 per person, $40,000 per accident for bodily injury, $15,000 for uninsured motorist property damage. Uninsured motorist bodily injury coverage includes underinsured motorist bodily injury coverage. You may not reject this coverage in writing. Your insurance company is required to offer you uninsured motorist bodily injury at higher limits — you may waive the higher coverage in writing.

MASSACHUSETTS

Minimum liability limits: $20,000 per person, $40,000 per accident for bodily injury liability, $5,000 per accident for property damage liability. You may also place $10,000 on deposit with the Division of Motor Vehicles in lieu of purchasing an insurance policy.

Minimum personal injury protection coverage: $2,000 for medical expenses, 75 percent of lost wages, $8,000 for replacement services, $2,000 for funeral expenses. The total of all coverages is subject to an $8,000 maximum when personal injury protection is purchased at the minimum limits.

Minimum uninsured motorist limits: $20,000 per person, $40,000 per accident for bodily injury. Uninsured motorist bodily injury coverage includes underinsured motorist bodily injury coverage. You may not reject this coverage.

MICHIGAN

Minimum liability limits: $20,000 per person, $40,000 per accident for bodily injury liability, $10,000 per accident for property damage liability. You may also use other forms of financial security approved by the Secretary of State in lieu of purchasing an insurance policy. If you own more than 25 vehicles, you may claim a self-insurance exemption from the insurance, bond, or deposit requirement. There is no self-insurance exemption available for individuals who own less than 25 vehicles.

Minimum personal injury protection coverage: Unlimited medical expenses, 85 percent of lost wages for three years, $20 per day for three years for replacement services, survivor benefits equal to lost wages and replacement services benefits, $1,750 for funeral expenses.

Minimum uninsured motorist limits: Michigan does not have any stated provisions for uninsured motorist bodily injury or uninsured motorist property damage coverage. Your insurer is not required to offer you these coverages, so no rejection is required.

MINNESOTA

Minimum liability limits: $30,000 per person, $60,000 per accident for bodily injury liability, $10,000 per accident for property damage liability. In certain circumstances, you may claim a self-insurance exemption from the insurance, bond, or deposit requirement.

Minimum personal injury protection coverage: $20,000 for medical expenses, 85 percent of lost wages, $200 per week for replacement services, $200 per week for survivor benefits, $2,000 for funeral expenses. The total of all coverages is subject to a limit of $40,000, and the total of all coverages other than for medical expenses is subject to a limit of $20,000, when minimum personal injury protection coverage is purchased.

Minimum uninsured motorist limits: $25,000 per person, $50,000 per accident for bodily injury. You may not reject this coverage. Minimum underinsured motorist limits: $25,000 per person, $50,000 per accident for underinsured motorist bodily injury. You may not reject this coverage.

MISSISSIPPI

Minimum liability limits: $25,000 per person, $50,000 per accident for bodily injury liability, $25,000 per accident for property damage liability. You may also purchase a $25,000 bond or place $25,000 on deposit with the Division of Motor Vehicles in lieu of purchasing an insurance policy. If you own more than 25 vehicles, you may claim a self-insurance exemption from the insurance, bond, or deposit requirement. Mississippi is not a no-fault state and does not allow insurers to offer personal injury protection coverage.

Minimum uninsured motorist limits: $25,000 per person, $50,000 per

accident for bodily injury, $25,000 for uninsured motorist property damage. Uninsured motorist bodily injury coverage includes underinsured motorist bodily injury coverage. You may reject this coverage in writing.

MISSOURI

Minimum liability limits: $25,000 per person, $50,000 per accident for bodily injury liability, $10,000 per accident for property damage liability. You may also place $60,000 on deposit with the Division of Motor Vehicles in lieu of purchasing an insurance policy. If you own more than 25 vehicles, you may claim a self-insurance exemption from the insurance, bond, or deposit requirement. Missouri is not a no-fault state and does not allow insurers to offer personal injury protection coverage.

Minimum uninsured motorist limits: $25,000 per person, $50,000 per accident for bodily injury. You may not reject this coverage. There are no stated provisions for uninsured motorist property damage coverage — your insurance company is not required to offer this coverage to you, so no rejection is required.

MONTANA

Minimum liability limits: $25,000 per person, $50,000 per accident for bodily injury liability, $10,000 per accident for property damage liability. You may also purchase a bond or place a deposit with the Division of Motor Vehicles in lieu of purchasing an insurance policy. If you own more than 25 vehicles, you may claim a self-insurance exemption from the insurance, bond, or deposit requirement. Montana is not a no-fault state and does not allow insurers to offer personal injury protection coverage.

Minimum uninsured motorist limits: $25,000 per person, $50,000 per accident for bodily injury. You may reject this coverage in writing. There are no stated provisions for uninsured motorist property damage coverage — your insurance company is not required to offer this coverage to you, so no rejection is required.

NEBRASKA

Minimum liability limits: $25,000 per person, $50,000 per accident for bodily injury liability, $25,000 per accident for property damage liability. You may also place $75,000 on deposit with the Division of Motor Vehicles in lieu of purchasing an insurance policy. If you own more than 25 vehicles, you may claim a self-insurance exemption from the insurance, bond, or deposit requirement. Nebraska is not a no-fault state and does not allow insurers to offer personal injury protection coverage.

Minimum uninsured motorist limits: $25,000 per person, $50,000 per accident for bodily injury. You may not reject this coverage. There are no stated provisions for uninsured motorist property damage coverage — your insurance company is not required to offer this coverage to you, so no rejection is required. Minimum underinsured motorist limits: $25,000 per person, $50,000 per accident for underinsured motorist bodily injury coverage. You may not reject this coverage.

NEVADA

Minimum liability limits: $15,000 per person, $30,000 per accident for bodily injury liability, $10,000 per accident for property damage liability. If you own more than ten vehicles, you may claim a self-insurance exemption from the insurance, bond, or deposit requirement. Nevada is not a no-fault state and does not allow insurers to offer personal injury protection coverage.

Minimum uninsured motorist limits: $15,000 per person, $30,000 per

accident for bodily injury. You may reject this coverage in writing. There are no stated provisions for uninsured motorist property damage coverage — your insurance company is not required to offer this coverage to you, so no rejection is required.

NEW HAMPSHIRE

New Hampshire is not a compulsory insurance state; thus, there are no minimum coverage limits.

NEW JERSEY

Minimum liability limits: $15,000 per person, $30,000 per accident for bodily injury liability, $5,000 per accident for property damage liability. If you own more than 25 vehicles, you may claim a self-insurance exemption from the insurance requirement.

Minimum personal injury protection coverage: $250,000 per person for medical expenses; $100 per week for lost wages; $12 per day for replacement services, subject to a lifetime maximum of $4,380; survivor benefits equal to lost wages and replacement services benefits, less any benefits received by the victim; $1,000 for funeral expenses.

Minimum uninsured motorist limits: $15,000 per person, $30,000 per accident for bodily injury, $5,000 for uninsured motorist property damage. You may not reject uninsured motorist bodily injury coverage. Minimum underinsured motorist limits: $15,000 per person, $30,000 per accident for underinsured motorist bodily injury coverage. You may not reject this coverage.

NEW MEXICO

Minimum liability limits: $25,000 per person, $50,000 per accident for bodily injury liability, $10,000 per accident for property damage liability. You may also purchase a $60,000 bond or place $60,000 on deposit with the Division of Motor Vehicles in lieu of purchasing an insurance policy. In certain circumstances, you may claim a self-insurance exemption from the insurance, bond, or deposit requirement. New Mexico is not a no-fault state and does not allow insurers to offer personal injury protection coverage.

Minimum uninsured motorist limits: $25,000 per person, $50,000 per accident for bodily injury, $10,000 for uninsured motorist property damage. Uninsured motorist bodily injury coverage includes underinsured motorist bodily injury coverage. You may reject this coverage in writing.

NEW YORK

Minimum liability limits: $25,000 per person, $50,000 per accident for bodily injury liability, $10,000 per accident for property damage liability, $50,000 per person, $100,000 per accident for wrongful death liability. You may also purchase a bond or place a $25,000 deposit with the Division of Motor Vehicles in lieu of purchasing an insurance policy. If you own more than 25 vehicles, you may claim a self-insurance exemption from the insurance, bond, or deposit requirement.

Minimum personal injury protection coverage: Unlimited medical expenses for one year, 80 percent of lost wages up to $2,000 per month for up to three years, $25 per day for replacement services for one year, survivor benefit of $2,000. The total of all coverages is subject to a limit of $50,000 if minimum personal injury protection limits are purchased.

Minimum uninsured motorist limits: $25,000 per person, $50,000 per accident for bodily injury, plus $50,000 per person, $100,000 per accident for wrongful death. You may not reject this coverage. There are no stated provisions for uninsured motorist property damage coverage — your insurance company is not required to offer this coverage to you, so no rejection is required.

NORTH CAROLINA

Minimum liability limits: $30,000 per person, $60,000 per accident for bodily injury liability, $25,000 per accident for property damage liability. You may also purchase a bond equal to the amount of the minimum bodily injury and property damage liability limits or place $85,000 on deposit with the Division of Motor Vehicles in lieu of purchasing an insurance policy. If you own more than 25 vehicles, you may claim a self-insurance exemption from the insurance, bond, or deposit requirement. North Carolina is not a no-fault state and does not allow insurers to offer personal injury protection coverage.

Minimum uninsured motorist limits: $30,000 per person, $60,000 per accident for bodily injury, $25,000 for uninsured motorist property damage. You may reject this coverage in writing. Minimum underinsured motorist limits: $30,000 per person, $60,000 per accident for underinsured motorist bodily injury coverage. Underinsured motorist bodily injury is mandatory on policies with uninsured motorist limits greater than the minimum limits and cannot be rejected on these policies.

NORTH DAKOTA

Minimum liability limits: $25,000 per person, $50,000 per accident for bodily injury liability, $25,000 per accident for property damage liability. In certain circumstances, you may claim a self-insurance exemption from the insurance, bond, or deposit requirement.

Minimum personal injury protection coverage: $30,000 for medical expenses, 85 percent of lost wages up to $150 per week, $15 per day for replacement services, $15 per day for survivor benefits, $3,500 for funeral expenses. The total of all coverages is subject to a $30,000 limit if minimum personal injury protection limits are purchased.

Minimum uninsured motorist limits: $25,000 per person, $50,000 per accident for bodily injury. You may not reject this coverage. There are no stated provisions for uninsured motorist property damage coverage — your insurance company is not required to offer this coverage to you, so no rejection is required. Minimum underinsured motorist limits: $25,000 per person, $50,000 per accident for underinsured motorist bodily injury coverage. You may not reject this coverage.

OHIO

Minimum liability limits: $12,500 per person, $25,000 per accident for bodily injury liability, $7,500 per accident for property damage liability. You may also purchase a $30,000 bond or place $30,000 on deposit with the Bureau of Motor Vehicles in lieu of purchasing an insurance policy. If you own more than 25 vehicles, you may claim a self-insurance exemption from the insurance, bond, or deposit requirement. Ohio is not a no-fault state and does not allow insurers to offer personal injury protection coverage.

Minimum uninsured motorist limits: $12,500 per person, $25,000 per accident for bodily injury, $7,500 for uninsured motorist property damage. Your insurance company is not required to offer uninsured motorist bodily injury coverage but is required to make uninsured motorist property damage coverage available on your request.

OKLAHOMA

Minimum liability limits: $25,000 per person, $50,000 per accident for bodily injury liability, $25,000 per accident for property damage liability. You may also purchase a bond in an amount equal to the minimum bodily injury and property damage liability limits or place $75,000 on deposit with the Division of Motor Vehicles in lieu of purchasing an insurance policy. If you own more than 25 vehicles, you may claim a self-insurance exemption from the insurance, bond, or deposit requirement. Oklahoma is not a no-fault state and does not allow insurers to offer personal injury protection coverage.

Minimum uninsured motorist limits: $25,000 per person, $50,000 per accident for bodily injury. You may reject this coverage in writing. Uninsured motorist bodily injury coverage includes underinsured motorist bodily injury coverage. There are no stated provisions for uninsured motorist property damage coverage — your insurance company is not required to offer this coverage to you, so no rejection is required.

OREGON

Minimum liability limits: $25,000 per person, $50,000 per accident for bodily injury liability, $10,000 per accident for property damage liability. If you own more than 25 vehicles, you may claim a self-insurance exemption from the insurance, bond, or deposit requirement.

Minimum personal injury protection coverage: $15,000 per person for medical expenses incurred within one year; 70 percent of lost wages up to $1,250 per month for one year; $5,000 for funeral expenses; $25 per day, up to $750 total, for child care services.

Minimum uninsured motorist limits: $25,000 per person, $50,000 per accident for bodily injury, $10,000 for uninsured motorist property damage. You may not reject uninsured motorist bodily injury coverage; however, you may reject uninsured motorist property damage coverage in writing. Minimum underinsured motorist limits: Must be equal to your uninsured motorist bodily injury limits. You may not reject this coverage if your uninsured motorist bodily injury limits are higher than the minimum bodily injury liability limits.

PENNSYLVANIA

Minimum liability limits: $15,000 per person, $30,000 per accident for bodily injury liability, $5,000 per accident for property damage liability. In certain circumstances, you may claim a self-insurance exemption from the insurance, bond, or deposit requirement.

Minimum personal injury protection coverage: $5,000 per person for medical expenses incurred within 18 months, 80 percent of lost wages. Your insurance company must also offer coverages that include payment for medical expenses up to $100,000; $1,100,000 for extraordinary medical expenses; lost wages of $2,500 per month, up to $50,000; $25,000 for accidental death benefits; $2,500 for funeral expenses. Combined optional benefits may be subject to a total limit of $177,500.

Minimum uninsured motorist limits: $15,000 per person, $30,000 per accident for bodily injury. You may reject this coverage in writing. There are no stated provisions for uninsured motorist property damage coverage — your insurance company is not required to offer this coverage to you, so no rejection is required. Minimum underinsured motorist limits: $15,000 per person, $30,000 per accident for underinsured motorist bodily injury coverage. You may reject this coverage in writing.

RHODE ISLAND

Minimum liability limits: $25,000 per person, $50,000 per accident for bodily injury liability, $25,000 per accident for property damage liability. You may also purchase a combined single limit policy with a minimum limit of $75,000. You may also purchase a bond or place $75,000 on deposit with the Division of Motor Vehicles in lieu of purchasing an insurance policy. If you own more than 25 vehicles, you may claim a self-insurance exemption from the insurance, bond, or deposit requirement. Rhode Island is not a no-fault state and does not allow insurers to offer personal injury protection coverage.

Minimum uninsured motorist limits: $25,000 per person, $50,000 per accident for bodily injury, $25,000 per accident for uninsured motorist property damage. You may reject this coverage in writing. Uninsured motorist bodily injury coverage includes underinsured motorist bodily injury coverage.

SOUTH CAROLINA

Minimum liability limits: $25,000 per person, $50,000 per accident for bodily injury liability, $25,000 per accident for property damage liability. You may also purchase a bond or place $35,000 on deposit with the Division of Motor Vehicles in lieu of purchasing an insurance policy. If you own more than 25 vehicles, you may claim a self-insurance exemption from the insurance, bond, or deposit requirement. South Carolina is not a no-fault state and does not allow insurers to offer personal injury protection coverage.

Minimum uninsured motorist limits: $25,000 per person, $50,000 per accident for bodily injury, $25,000 per accident for uninsured motorist property damage coverage. You may not reject uninsured motorist bodily injury; however, you may reject uninsured motorist property damage coverage in writing. Minimum underinsured motorist limits: $25,000 per person, $50,000 per accident for underinsured motorist bodily injury coverage. You may reject this coverage in writing.

SOUTH DAKOTA

Minimum liability limits: $25,000 per person, $50,000 per accident for bodily injury liability, $25,000 per accident for property damage liability. You may also purchase a bond or place $25,000 on deposit with the Division of Motor Vehicles in lieu of purchasing an insurance policy. If you own more than 25 vehicles, you may claim a self-insurance exemption from the insurance, bond, or deposit requirement.

Minimum personal injury protection coverage: $2,000 per person for medical expenses, $60 per week for one year for lost wages, $10,000 for survivor benefits.

Minimum uninsured motorist limits: $25,000 per person, $50,000 per accident for bodily injury. You may not reject this coverage. There are no stated provisions for uninsured motorist property damage coverage — your insurance company is not required to offer this coverage to you, so no rejection is required. Minimum underinsured motorist limits: $25,000 per person, $50,000 per accident for underinsured motorist bodily injury. You may not reject this coverage.

TENNESSEE

Minimum liability limits: $25,000 per person, $50,000 per accident for bodily injury liability, $10,000 per accident for property damage liability. You can purchase a combined single limit policy with a minimum limit of $60,000. You may also purchase a $60,000 bond or place $60,000 on deposit with the Division of Motor Vehicles in lieu of purchasing an insurance policy. If you own more than 25 vehicles, you may claim a self-insurance exemption from the insurance, bond, or deposit requirement. Tennessee is not a no-fault state and does not allow insurers to offer personal injury protection coverage.

Minimum uninsured motorist limits: $25,000 per person, $50,000 per accident for bodily injury (or $60,000 combined single limit), $10,000 per accident for uninsured motorist property damage. You may reject this coverage in writing. Uninsured motorist bodily injury coverage includes underinsured motorist bodily injury coverage.

TEXAS

Minimum liability limits: $20,000 per person, $40,000 per accident for bodily injury liability, $15,000 per accident for property damage liability. You may also purchase a bond or place $55,000 on deposit with the Division of Motor Vehicles in lieu of purchasing an insurance policy. If you own more than 25 vehicles, you may claim a self-insurance exemption from the insurance, bond, or deposit requirement.

Minimum personal injury protection coverage: $2,500 for a combination of medical expenses, lost wages, and replacement services.

Minimum uninsured motorist limits: $20,000 per person, $40,000 per accident for bodily injury, $15,000 per accident for property damage. You may reject this coverage in writing. Minimum underinsured motorist limits: $20,000 per person, $40,000 per accident for underinsured motorist bodily injury coverage. You may reject this coverage in writing.

UTAH

Minimum liability limits: $25,000 per person, $50,000 per accident for bodily injury liability, $15,000 per accident for property damage liability. You may purchase a combined single limit policy with a minimum limit of $65,000. You may also purchase a bond or place $135,000 on deposit with the Division of Motor Vehicles in lieu of purchasing an insurance policy. If you own more than 24 vehicles and place a deposit with the Division of Motor Vehicles, you may claim a self-insurance exemption from the insurance, bond, or $135,000 deposit requirement.

Minimum personal injury protection coverage: $3,000 for medical expenses, $250 per week or 85 percent of lost wages for one year, $25 per day for one year for replacement services, $1,500 per person for funeral expenses, $3,000 for survivor benefits.

Minimum uninsured motorist limits: $25,000 per person, $50,000 per accident (or $65,000 combined single limit) for bodily injury, the actual cash value of the vehicle or $3,500 (whichever is less) for uninsured motorist property damage. You may reject uninsured motorist bodily injury coverage in writing. You may reject uninsured motorist property damage coverage only if you have purchased collision coverage; otherwise, this coverage is mandatory. Minimum underinsured motorist limits: $10,000 per person, $20,000 per accident for underinsured motorist bodily injury. You may reject this coverage in writing.

VERMONT

Minimum liability limits: $25,000 per person, $50,000 per accident for bodily injury liability, $10,000 per accident for property damage liability. If you have $115,000 available for bodily injury and property damage liability, you may claim a self-insurance exemption from the insurance requirement. Vermont is not a no-fault state and does not allow insurers to offer personal injury protection coverage.

Minimum uninsured motorist limits: $25,000 per person, $50,000 per accident for bodily injury, $10,000 per accident for uninsured motorist property damage. You may not reject uninsured motorist bodily injury coverage or uninsured motorist property damage coverage. Uninsured motorist bodily injury coverage includes underinsured motorist bodily injury coverage.

VIRGINIA

Minimum liability limits: $25,000 per person, $50,000 per accident for bodily injury liability, $20,000 per accident for property damage liability. You may also purchase a bond or place a deposit with the Division of Motor Vehicles in lieu of purchasing an insurance policy. If you own more than 20 vehicles, you may claim a self-insurance exemption from the insurance, bond, or deposit requirement. If you do not purchase an insurance policy, you must pay a $500 uninsured motorist fee to register your vehicle.

Minimum personal injury protection coverage: $2,000 per person for medical and funeral expenses, $100 per week for lost wages for one year.

Minimum uninsured motorist limits: $25,000 per person, $50,000 per accident for bodily injury, $20,000 per accident for uninsured motorist property damage. You may not reject this coverage in writing. Uninsured motorist bodily injury coverage includes underinsured motorist bodily injury coverage.

WASHINGTON

Minimum liability limits: $25,000 per person, $50,000 per accident for bodily injury liability, $10,000 per accident for property damage liability. You may also deposit a $55,000 Certificate of Deposit with the Division of Motor Vehicles in lieu of purchasing an insurance policy. If you own more than 25 vehicles, you may claim a self-insurance exemption from the insurance, bond, or deposit requirement.

Minimum personal injury protection coverage: $10,000 for medical and hospital expenses; $200 per week for lost wages, up to $10,000; $200 per week for replacement services, up to $5,000; $2,000 for funeral expenses.

Minimum uninsured motorist limits: $25,000 per person, $50,000 per accident for bodily injury, $10,000 per accident for uninsured motorist property damage. You may reject uninsured motorist bodily injury coverage in writing; however, you may reject uninsured motorist property damage coverage only if you have purchased comprehensive and collision coverage. Uninsured motorist bodily injury coverage includes underinsured motorist bodily injury coverage.

WEST VIRGINIA

Minimum liability limits: $20,000 per person, $40,000 per accident for bodily injury liability, $10,000 per accident for property damage liability. You may also place $40,000 on deposit with the Division of Motor Vehicles in lieu of purchasing an insurance policy. If you own more than 25 vehicles, you may claim a self-insurance exemption from the insurance, bond, or deposit requirement. West Virginia is not a no-fault state and does not allow insurers to offer personal injury protection coverage.

Minimum uninsured motorist limits: $20,000 per person, $40,000 per accident for bodily injury, $10,000 per accident for property damage. You may not reject this coverage. Minimum underinsured motorist limits: $20,000 per person, $40,000 per accident for underinsured motorist bodily injury coverage. You may reject this coverage in writing.

WISCONSIN

Wisconsin is not a compulsory insurance state; thus, there are no minimum coverage requirements.

WYOMING

Minimum liability limits: $25,000 per person, $50,000 per accident for bodily injury liability, $20,000 per accident for property damage liability. You may also purchase a bond in an amount equal to the minimum bodily injury and property damage liability limits or place $25,000 on deposit with the Division of Motor Vehicles in lieu of purchasing an insurance policy. If you own more than 25 vehicles, you may claim a self-insurance exemption from the insurance, bond, or deposit requirement. Wyoming is not a no-fault state and does not allow insurers to offer personal injury protection coverage.

Minimum uninsured motorist limits: $25,000 per person, $50,000 per accident for bodily injury, $20,000 per accident for property damage. You may reject this coverage in writing. Uninsured motorist bodily injury coverage includes underinsured motorist bodily injury coverage.

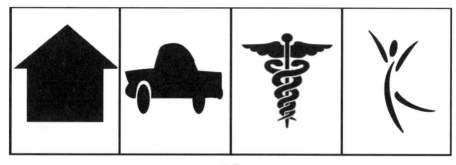

13

BASIC AUTOMOBILE INSURANCE POLICIES

This chapter will describe the most common types of auto insurance policies offered by insurance companies and help you decide which type of policy is right for you.

BASIC LIABILITY POLICIES

A basic liability policy is designed to make sure you comply with your state's financial responsibility laws but offers little or no compensation for you if you are injured or if your property is damaged in an accident. This type of policy is designed to minimize your policy premiums.

Different insurance companies have different definitions of a basic liability package. Some may offer you a basic policy with adequate bodily injury liability and property damage liability coverages but no comprehensive or collision coverage. Other companies will offer you only the minimum coverages and limits required by your state.

Because basic liability policies vary from company to company, it is important to know which coverages you are being offered when you are shopping for quotes. For example, let us suppose you are gathering quotes for an automobile insurance policy in Ohio. Company A quotes you for only the minimum state requirements — $12,500 per person, $25,000 per accident for bodily injury liability, and $7,500 for property damage liability. Company A is not required to offer you medical payments coverage, uninsured and underinsured motorist coverage, or physical damage coverages, such as comprehensive or collision. You are shopping to get the lowest possible rate, so you call Company B, who quotes you at state minimum liability limits but includes $1,000 in medical payments and includes uninsured and underinsured motorist for both bodily injury and property damage.

Company A's quote will be lower than Company B's because it has included much less coverage on your quote. If you choose to purchase an automobile insurance policy with Company A and you are in an accident with an uninsured motorist, you will not be able to receive any benefit from your policy to cover injuries that you or your passengers sustain as a result of the accident. With the limited coverages under your automobile insurance policy, neither will you receive any compensation for damage to your vehicle. If you had chosen Company B, you would have been able to benefit from the uninsured motorist coverage under your policy and would have been entitled to payment for the injuries and property you sustained as a result of the accident.

You can avoid being inadequately insured by asking questions when you are calling around for quotes. Ask the agent to go over what coverages they are quoting and ask about medical payments coverage and uninsured and underinsured motorist.

If you are purchasing a policy from an agency, be sure to sit down with the agent or associate you are starting your policy with. Ask the agent to review the coverages with you line by line, and ask questions on anything you do not understand before you purchase an automobile insurance policy. Insurance agents are required to take licensure classes and have to pass a test to obtain their license, and so they have spent a great deal of time acquiring information about insurance. If they cannot answer your questions immediately, most agents have the resources to call an underwriter or look up the answers to policy coverage questions.

It is also important to keep in mind that agents use insurance terms that may not make sense to policyholders, so it can be difficult to understand what your policy covers unless you ask questions. If they use insurance terminology that is unfamiliar to you, ask them to explain it in different terms so you can better understand the coverage.

FULL COVERAGE POLICIES

Full coverage policies are designed to provide protection that is greater than the state minimum, including coverage for your motor vehicle and personal property. Like basic liability policies, full coverage policy coverages vary from company to company, so it is important to compare several quotes before making a decision to purchase a policy through a certain insurance company. If you ask for full coverage on your motor vehicle, it is also important to ask questions about the coverages and limits being quoted.

When financing a vehicle, loan companies require that you carry comprehensive coverage, which covers losses such as glass damage, collision with an animal, theft, and vandalism, and collision coverage, which covers the collision with another object except for an animal.

Comprehensive and collision coverage can be assigned different deductibles.

For example, you could carry a $250 deductible on comprehensive and a $500 deductible on collision. The higher your deductible is, the lower your premiums. When choosing deductibles for comprehensive and collision coverage, you must consider how much money you could reasonably pay out of pocket if your car was wrecked or stolen.

Some companies will automatically quote coverage for towing and rental expenses. These coverages are inexpensive but could prove critical if your vehicle is damaged or disabled due to an accident. Most companies also include lock-out services in the towing portion coverage and will reimburse for towing even in the event of mechanical breakdown.

Let us now look at an example. You call Company A and tell them you just purchased a new vehicle and need full coverage insurance on the vehicle. Company A quotes you with state minimum liability, a deductible of $1,000 for both comprehensive and collision and no towing or rental. You then call Company B and ask for a full coverage quote. Company B quotes you at state minimum liability with a $250 deductible for comprehensive coverage and a $500 deductible for collision. It also adds towing and rental.

Company A is most likely going to come back with a lower rate, because it has quoted you with higher deductible amounts and has excluded towing and rental. Let us suppose that you choose Company A for its lower rate. One month later, you lose control of your car and hit a utility pole. You are not injured, but your car is not drivable.

When you call your insurance company to file a claim, you are advised that you have a $1,000 deductible you will have to pay before your vehicle can be repaired. You will not be able to come up with $1,000 for a few weeks. In the meantime, your automobile is disabled, and you have no transportation to and from work. You inquire about a rental car, but your insurance company advises you that you have no rental coverage under your policy. This leaves you with obtaining $1,000 to satisfy your deductible so that your vehicle can be repaired and the expense of renting a vehicle to drive to and from work. If you would have chosen Company B's quote, you would have to pay $500 to get your car fixed, but you would have a rental car to get you to and from work, with no extra out-of-pocket expense, while your car is being repaired.

TO ENSURE YOUR COVERAGE IS ADEQUATE

The best way to make sure you have adequate coverage is to be informed of what coverages are available under your automobile insurance policy and make sure you are being quoted the same coverages by every company so that you can obtain an accurate comparison.

You should take the time to consider what is at risk if you choose not to purchase each coverage at certain limits. You should take into account how much money you have available in your personal savings and investments to cover losses that may arise as a result of a motor vehicle accident, theft, or vandalism. If you caused an accident, would you have sufficient funds to pay for the bodily injuries or damage to personal property you may cause to others? If you are in an accident, would your health insurance coverage be sufficient to pay for your injuries, and would you have adequate cash reserves to pay for damage to your automobile and personal property? If you were struck by an uninsured motorist, would you be able to pay for your medical bills and for repairs to your motor vehicle?

You should not only consider the financial reserves you have available, but also the requirements your lender may place on you if you have financed or leased your motor vehicle. Many lenders require that you carry certain liability limits and comprehensive and collision coverage to protect the lender's financial interests in the event of an accident or other loss.

Although some companies will quote you inexpensive rates for automobile insurance, they may not provide policies with coverages that meet your needs. If you have an idea of what deductibles you want, what liability limits you are comfortable with, whether you need uninsured and underinsured motorist protection, or whether you would need help paying for towing and rental car expenses in the event of an accident or loss, you will be better prepared to discuss coverages with your agent or insurance company to make sure you purchase a policy that meets your financial needs.

Few things are more stressful than filing a claim and finding out you do not have adequate coverage. After the accident has happened and the claim has been filed, it is too late to add coverage or reduce deductibles. Many people believe they will never be involved in an accident until it happens. Being informed about what your policy does and does not cover from the beginning is the best way to save yourself from a bad financial situation.

Once you know what coverage options you need to financially protect yourself and your family, you can have each company you call quote the limits and coverages you have decided on and then choose the most economical quote. It is important to always remember that the insurance policy with the cheapest monthly payment available does not always provide the best coverage to protect you and your family. If you are in an accident and do not have adequate coverage, you could potentially end up in a financially disastrous situation.

In the next chapter, you will learn about ways to save money on your automobile insurance policy while obtaining the coverage you need.

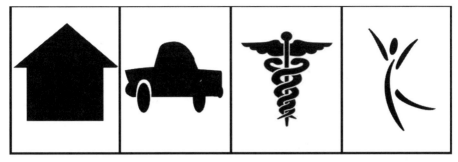

14

HOW TO SHOP FOR CHEAP AUTO INSURANCE

In the last chapter, you learned about the techniques for comparing policy coverages to make sure you are getting quotes on similar coverage with each company. This chapter will explore additional techniques for shopping around for the lowest rate.

As with home insurance, it is helpful to use an independent agent. With an independent agent, you can discuss the coverages you need with one person and get multiple quotes for automobile insurance policies in the same time it takes to contact a captive agent to obtain a single quote from a single company. This technique will save you time and minimize the legwork that comes with calling every company listed in the phone book. Your agent will also be able to assure you that you are being quoted the same coverages on each quote.

If you decide to go through the phone book and call as many insurance agents as possible, keep a list of what company they represent. This will help you avoid calling more than one agent from the same company, resulting in a duplicate quote.

One technique you may find helpful is making a list of the deductible amounts, liability limits, and additional coverages you need so you can ask each agent for the same quoted coverage. You also need to keep a list of drivers in your household with the birth date, license number, and social security number for each driver. You should also write down the Vehicle Identification Number (VIN) for each vehicle you own. Not all companies ask the same questions, but it will save you time and having to call agents back with information if you keep the information readily available.

If you are not comfortable getting a quote over the phone, you can walk into an insurance agency to get a quote. If you decide to shop for quotes this way, be sure to have all your personal and driver information, as well as your VIN numbers available. You can find an agent in your area by searching online, checking the yellow pages, or asking your friends and family whom they have their insurance with. It is also helpful to take the declarations page for your current insurance company with you if you already have insurance. The declarations page will show all the coverages you currently have and will often list the Vehicle Identification Number for each vehicle covered by your current policy.

You may also find it helpful to make a list of any questions you have before going to the agent's office. It is often easy to forget the questions you may have had when you get on the phone or to the agent's office. Having a list ready to check off will help assure you that you understand what is covered and what is not and that you are being quoted for adequate coverage limits.

Do not be afraid to ask questions. If you do not ask questions, you may not find out that your coverage is inadequate until you have to file a claim. Being involved in an accident is stressful enough without having to worry about paying for a rental car or not being able to pay the necessary deductible to get your car fixed. An insurance agent who has been in the business any time has most likely heard every question at least once or twice, so do not be afraid to ask no matter how stupid you believe your question is.

Many insurance agencies have the ability to print off quotes or e-mail quotes to you. It is helpful, when determining which quote to purchase, to compare coverage line by line. Having printed copies of each quote can help you keep track of each quote you have received and will give you a hard copy to review at your leisure.

Do not wait until the last minute to purchase insurance. If you are purchasing a car for the first time, do not wait until you are sitting at a car dealership purchasing your vehicle. Auto dealerships often have a referral network set up with a few different agents, but they may not be able to provide the lowest quote or the most advantageous coverage. Instead, when you begin car shopping, get an idea of what year, make, and models you are interested in and compare quotes on the different types of vehicles. If you look at a vehicle you are interested in purchasing, you may be able to secure the VIN number from the dealership so you can get quotes before buying the vehicle. This practice will also give you a realistic idea of what the rates will be on different vehicles, and you can factor in the cost of insurance when making the final decision on the vehicle you want to purchase.

Another way to find cheap insurance is to use the Internet. There are Internet companies that give you an online form to fill out. These companies will then sell your information to different insurance companies or agencies, and the agents will call you back with the quote. This can save you the time of having to call different companies. If you use this technique to shop for automobile insurance, keep a list of questions you want to ask located near the phone so you will be prepared when these agents start calling you.

Keep your insurance declarations pages on file. Some insurance companies will discount your rate or offer standard or preferred rating if you can show proof of prior insurance. By keeping your declarations pages filed together in a specific location you will be able to provide the proof of insurance that your new company requires. You will also have them available when comparing quotes with new companies to make sure you are not getting a reduction in coverage along with a reduction in price.

It is best to start shopping before your policy renews. Most companies will charge you for the coverage you have had between your last payment and your cancellation dates. Some companies will charge you an extra fee for canceling mid-term. If possible, it is always best to switch insurance companies at renewal to avoid any additional fees.

If you are not satisfied with the claims handling, customer service, or other aspects of your current company and do not want to wait until renewal to cancel your policy, ask your agent if any penalty fees for canceling mid-term will be added. Many insurance companies levy hefty fees on policies that are canceled at the request of the insured for any reason other than disposal of the insured vehicle, voluntary forfeiture of an insured person's driver license, or relocation of the named insured to another state. In some states, insurance companies are permitted to assess fees equal to 10 percent of the unearned policy premium.

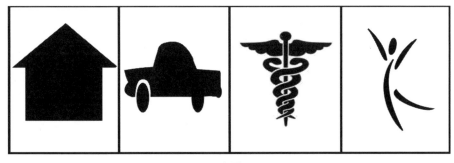

15

THE AUTOMOBILE INSURANCE POINT SYSTEM

One of the most important techniques for reducing the cost of your automobile insurance is to reduce the number of violations and accidents on your driving record and to make sure your driver's license is valid. This chapter will explain how the automobile insurance point system works and how violations and accidents on your driving record can affect the premiums you pay for automobile insurance coverage.

Insurance companies use many factors to determine your automobile insurance premiums, but one of the factors that can most dramatically affect your rates is violation and accident information that the insurance company obtains from your motor vehicle report and CLUE report.

Most insurance companies assign points for violations and accidents and assign a factor for each point value. The number of points assigned to each driver on an insurance policy does not necessarily correspond directly to the number of points assigned for the violations and accidents by the Department of Motor Vehicles of your state. Your insurance company may weigh violations or accidents more or less heavily than the Department of Motor Vehicles.

Your insurance agent should be able to give you a table showing how the insurance company assigns points for violations and accidents. This will give you an idea of how your insurance company rates your policy based on traffic violations and motor vehicle accidents. If your agent does not have access to this information, keep in mind that these tables are public record and can be obtained from the Department of Motor Vehicles of your state.

Here is an example of how your motor vehicle report and CLUE report can affect your premiums for automobile insurance: Let us suppose two drivers are the same age and gender, drive the same type of vehicle, and live in the same rating territory. The first driver has a clean driving record, with no violations or accidents for the past three years. The second driver has incurred two speeding tickets and had one at-fault accident in the same time period.

Both drivers apply for insurance through the same insurance company. Let us suppose that the total policy premium for each driver is $400 for a six-month policy term before information from driving records and CLUE reports is factored in.

The first driver would have a total policy premium of $400, because there are no violations or accidents to factor in. Since the second driver has two violations and one accident on his or her driving record, the insurance company would determine the point values for both occurrences before calculating the final policy premium.

Suppose that the insurance company charges one point for speeding tickets, three points for at-fault accidents, and that the company adds a factor of 10 percent for each point — that is, the premium increases by 10 percent for each point derived from information on a driver's motor vehicle report or CLUE report.

The insurance company would assign a total of five points to the policy for the second driver — one for each of the speeding tickets and three for the at-fault accident. Thus, the total policy premium of $400 for the second driver would be multiplied by a total point factor of 1.5. This driver would pay $600 for the same coverage as the first driver. With a few occurrences on the second driver's records, this driver will pay 50 percent more than the first driver.

If you have a clean driving record, you will obtain a substantially lower policy premium than a driver with a few blemishes on his or her record. Of course, there is no easy way to repair this if you already have a few violations on your record. The best way to save money if you already have violations or accidents on your record is to be honest with each insurance agent or company from which you obtain a quote. If you are not sure how many violations or accidents are on your driving record, take the time to obtain a copy of your motor vehicle report and your CLUE report before you begin the process of obtaining quotes for automobile insurance coverage. This will help to ensure that you are giving accurate information to each insurance agent and help you obtain accurate quotes.

Making sure each insurance agent knows about every accident and violation on your driving record is the only way to effectively compare quotes and obtain the best coverage at the lowest premium rates. Many drivers do not tell agents about violations or accidents, thinking the insurance company will not find out about these occurrences. You will find, though, that even if an insurance company is willing to issue an automobile insurance policy before obtaining motor vehicle reports and CLUE reports, the company will substantially raise your rates or even rescind your policy (cancel it back to inception, as if the insurance policy had never existed) once it receives the reports if you do not disclose all of your violations and accidents on your application.

The good news about violations and accidents is the majority of insurance companies consider information only less than three years old. Once information on your motor vehicle report and CLUE report is more than three years old, these insurance companies will remove the points associated with that information from your policy at renewal, resulting in a lower premium rate for your automobile insurance policy.

Working to improve your driving record is one of the best ways to reduce the amount you pay for automobile insurance over the long term. Make sure you pay attention to posted speed limits, obey stop signs and traffic signals, and avoid activities that lead to accidents, such as eating, smoking, or other distracting activities, while operating a motor vehicle.

Some states will allow you to remove a certain number of points from your driving record if you attend a defensive driving course after incurring a motor vehicle violation. This course lasts only one day and is sometimes just a few hours. If your state has this type of defensive driving course available, it may be worth the time so that you can reduce your automobile insurance premiums. If you choose to take a driving course to remove points from your driving record, be sure to provide your agent with a copy of the certificate you receive on completion of the course so your rates can be adjusted.

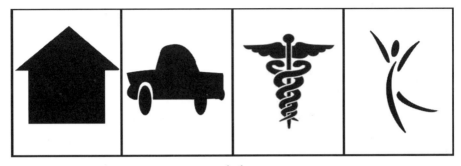

16

USING DISCOUNTS
TO SAVE MONEY
ON AUTOMOBILE
INSURANCE

Aside from keeping a clean driving record, one of the best ways to save money on automobile insurance is to make sure all applicable discounts are applied to your quote or policy premiums. Although some agents will tell you about all the available discounts to help you reduce your premiums, there are many less experienced agents who may not alert you to all these discounts. It is a good idea to ask about each discount you believe you may qualify for. You may have to provide documentation to receive some of the discounts, such as an anti-theft device discount for a device installed after the car was manufactured, but the money you save on your automobile insurance is worth the trouble of obtaining the documentation.

Here is a list of discounts that many insurance companies offer on their automobile insurance policies. Not every insurance company will offer every discount, and there may be additional discounts mandated by your state.

Airbags. Your insurance company may provide a discount if your motor vehicle has front airbags and may provide an additional discount if the vehicle has side curtain airbags. This discount runs between 5 and 10 percent off your policy premiums. Since all vehicles manufactured since 1991 have airbags, it is likely that insurance companies will stop offering this discount over the next decade. Insurance companies verify whether a vehicle has airbags and the type of airbags from information derived from the Vehicle Identification Number.

Anti-lock Brakes. If your motor vehicle is equipped with anti-lock brakes, you may be able to obtain a 5 to 10 percent discount off certain policy coverages. Insurance companies verify whether a vehicle has anti-lock brakes from information derived from the VIN.

Anti-theft Device. Many companies offer a discount if your vehicle is equipped with an anti-theft device. Some companies offer different levels of discounts for different types of anti-theft devices, based on data that indicates how effective each type of device is at deterring vehicle thefts. Depending on the type of anti-theft device your vehicle has, you could save as much as 15 to 20 percent off certain coverage premiums.

If your motor vehicle came from the manufacturer with an anti-theft device installed, your insurance company should be able to verify this via information contained in the Vehicle Identification Number. If your anti-theft device was installed after the vehicle was manufactured, you may need to provide your insurance company with proof that the device was installed, such as a copy of the sales and installation receipt from the company that installed your anti-theft device.

Claims-Free Renewal. Your insurance company may provide a discount for each successive policy term during which no claims were submitted for payment under your policy. This discount accrues over successive policy periods, so the longer you keep your insurance policy without submitting a claim, the higher your discount will be.

If you do submit a claim for payment, you may lose all claims-free renewal discounts you have accrued before the claim.

Daytime Running Lights. If your car is equipped with daytime running lights, which automatically turn on when the car is running regardless of whether it is dark or light outside, you may be eligible for a discount on your automobile insurance policy premiums. This discount can save you 5 to 10 percent on certain policy coverages.

Driver Improvement Course. Your insurance company may offer you a discount for completion of a driver improvement course administered by your state's Department of Motor Vehicles or similar entity. This discount is available only when you have taken the course voluntarily, instead of being forced to attend the course by a court.

Some states allow insurance companies to offer this discount to people only over a certain age (often 55 or 60), hoping that older drivers will use the discount as an incentive to attend a refresher course to sharpen their driving skills.

Good Student. Some insurance companies offer students a discount for maintaining good grades. The criteria and amount of the discount vary from company to company. If you or a driver in your household who is a student qualifies for this discount, you may need to submit a copy of a report card or transcript to your agent so your policy may be properly credited.

Homeowner. If you own your home, condominium, or trailer, you may be able to qualify for a discount on your automobile insurance premiums. The rationale behind this discount is that people who own homes are more financially responsible and less risk tolerant than people who do not own their homes. Regardless of whether this rationale is valid, you can take advantage of auto insurance savings if you own your home.

Multiple Line. If you have more than one type of policy with the same insurance company, such as an automobile policy and a homeowner's policy, you may be able to save money on both policies. Some companies offer a discount of 10 to 15 percent for policyholders who hold multiple policies with the same insurer.

Multiple Vehicle. If you insure more than one vehicle on the same policy, some insurance companies will offer you a discount on your policy premiums. This discount can be as much as 10 percent — an excellent way to save money on your automobile insurance premiums without having to do anything to obtain the savings.

New Business Transfer. Some companies, particularly those that serve both the standard and nonstandard insurance markets, offer discounts to applicants who currently have automobile insurance in force with another company. The rationale behind this discount is that if you currently have insurance through another company, you are demonstrating a level of responsibility that suggests you are a better risk than someone who does not possess automobile insurance. This discount may help you save 5 to 10 percent on certain policy coverages.

Passive Restraints. Some vehicles feature shoulder belts, called passive restraints, that automatically retract when the vehicle is started, eliminating the chance that front seat drivers will forget to fasten their safety belts. If your car has passive restraints, you may be able to save 5 percent or more on certain coverages. Insurance companies verify the presence of passive restraints via the VIN.

Paid in Full. Given the high cost of automobile insurance, many policyholders prefer to pay their premiums in monthly or bimonthly installments. Almost all insurance companies reward policyholders who choose to pay the premiums for each policy term in full, by offering a discount on policy premiums. An insurance company may offer a 5 percent discount for policyholders who pay their entire premiums at the beginning of each term.

VIN Etching. Some insurance companies offer discounts for VIN etching, a process by which the Vehicle Identification Number is etched onto each window of the vehicle. VIN etching is designed to reduce the number of vehicle thefts and make stolen vehicles easier to track down and recover. VIN etching is done on an aftermarket basis, so you may need to submit proof that your vehicle has had all its windows etched before you can receive this discount.

The more of these discounts you can qualify for, the greater your premium savings will be. It is possible to save up to 50 percent on your policy premiums just by taking advantage of discounts offered by your insurance company.

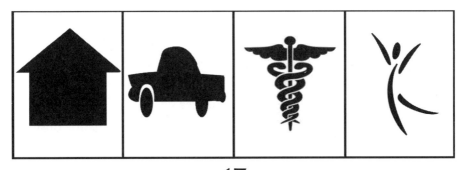

17

BEING AWARE OF SURCHARGES

Even if you are a careful driver, shop diligently for your automobile insurance policy, and ask your agent about available discounts, you may end up paying more than necessary for your automobile insurance coverage if your insurer adds a surcharge to your policy. Some states require that insurance companies disclose surcharges to policyholders in writing; however, these disclosures may not be easily located in your policy materials.

When you are shopping for an insurance policy or reviewing your policy coverages at renewal, take the time to find out if your insurance company will impose any surcharges on your policy. If your insurance company has added a surcharge to your policy premiums or plans to add a surcharge at renewal, ask your agent how much the surcharge affects your policy premiums, and find out what steps you need to take to have the surcharge removed from your policy.

Here are some of the most common surcharges used by automobile insurance companies:

BUSINESS USE

Many insurance companies will impose a surcharge if you use your motor vehicle for business use. Each company may have a different definition of business use — some consider your vehicle as being used for business use if you drive to more than one job site per day. Others may define business use as carrying tools or supplies for your job in your vehicle.

If you use your motor vehicle for any other purpose besides personal pleasure or commuting to work at a single location, you should ask your agent or insurance company what activities it considers to be business use. If your insurance company determines that your automobile is used for business use, it may impose a surcharge of an additional 10 to 20 percent of your policy premiums. This can add a significant cost to your personal automobile insurance premiums.

Also, some insurers consider certain activities to be commercial use, rather than business use. These activities include delivery of pizza or other foods to business or residential customers, transportation of clients for a fee, and hauling landscaping or heavy equipment, among other activities. If you are using your motor vehicle for activities that are considered commercial use by your automobile insurance company, you will not be eligible for coverage under a private passenger automobile insurance coverage. You will need to purchase a commercial automobile insurance policy to cover these types of activities.

FREQUENT INTERSTATE TRAVEL

If you frequently travel to another state, your insurance company may assess a surcharge against your policy — this surcharge may amount to 10 to 20 percent of your policy premiums.

The reason some companies levy this surcharge is because policy limits and mandatory coverages vary from state to state, and your automobile insurance company may be required to pay higher limits or different coverages than those stated on your declarations page if you are in an accident in another state. The surcharge allows the insurance company to offset the uncertainty created by this risk.

A common scenario that may cause you to be assessed a frequent interstate travel surcharge is working in a state different than the one in which you reside.

INEXPERIENCED OR YOUTHFUL DRIVER

Your insurance company may impose a surcharge on the premiums charged for a driver on your policy who does not have at least three years of driving experience. There are two reasons for this: First, individuals with less than a few years of driving experience are statistically more likely to be involved in an accident than drivers with substantial experience; second, the insurance company will have a limited driver history on which to base its premium rates for that person.

An inexperienced or youthful driver surcharge may add 10 to 20 percent to your automobile insurance rates.

INTERNATIONAL DRIVER'S LICENSE

If you have recently relocated to the United States from another country and have not yet obtained a United States driver's license, your automobile insurance company may impose a surcharge. This can add between 10 and 25 percent to your policy premiums.

The reason many insurers impose a surcharge if you have a driver's license issued by a country other than the United States is because your insurer will not be able to obtain your driving record from the country that issued your driver's license. The company will not be able to independently verify the accuracy of the driving history you reported on your automobile insurance application.

If an insurance company has assessed an international driver's license surcharge on your policy, the easiest way to lower your automobile insurance premium is to obtain a United States driver's license. Once you have done this, notify your insurance company as soon as possible so the surcharge can be removed from your policy.

SR-22

If your insurance company must file an SR-22 to show the Department of Motor Vehicles or the Department of Transportation that you carry at least the minimum insurance required by your state, the company may charge a fee for this filing. This fee is between $10 and $20. As long as you keep your policy in force with no lapses in coverage, your automobile insurance company will charge this fee only once.

UNVERIFIABLE DRIVER RECORD

This surcharge may be applied if your insurance company is unable to obtain a motor vehicle report, CLUE report, or other document showing a verifiable driving history for a person covered under your policy. An unverifiable driver record surcharge may add 10 to 20 percent to your automobile insurance costs.

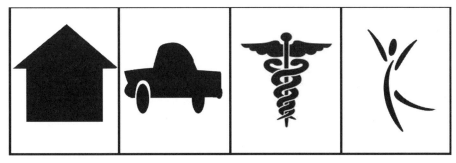

18

AUTOMOBILE
INSURANCE FEES

This chapter will detail fees your insurer may add to your policy. These fees can add significant costs to your personal automobile insurance. Here are some of the fees commonly assessed by automobile insurers:

ACQUISITION CHARGE

When you start a new policy with an insurance company, your company may charge you a portion of your first policy term's premiums to recoup advertising, administrative, and other costs associated with gaining you as a policyholder.

This charge can be spread out over the first policy term if you are on an installment payment plan.

CANCELLATION FEE

If you choose to cancel your automobile insurance policy during a policy term, do not expect to get all of your unused premiums back. Many insurance companies charge fees to policyholders who cancel their policies mid-term.

Depending on your state's insurance laws, your insurance company may be able to charge you for canceling your policy either by assessing a flat fee or returning your unused premiums on a pro-rata basis.

If the insurance company charges a flat fee, you may pay $25 or more for canceling your policy. If it charges on a pro-rata basis, it will calculate the number of days left in your policy term, determine the premiums it would have received for those days if you had not canceled your policy, and deduct 5 or 10 percent of that amount from any refund it owes to you.

Because a pro-rata cancellation fee depends on the number of days left in a policy term, this charge can be quite hefty if you cancel soon after beginning a policy term. If you cancel near the end of your policy term, however, your charge will be fairly low. Of course, if you are near the end of a policy term and want to switch automobile insurance companies, it is best to continue your coverage until the end of the term and elect not to renew your policy so that you will not be charged.

POLICY FEE

Similar to an acquisition charge, a policy fee is an amount you pay when you begin a new policy with an insurance company. The amounts for these fees vary depending on the company you choose, the program in which your insurance company places you, and the affiliate of an insurance company that underwrites your automobile insurance policy. Some companies do not charge a policy fee; others charge fees as high as $50 or more.

Depending on the company you choose to provide your automobile insurance, you may be required to pay the entire policy fee with your down payment, or the company may allow you to spread the fee over the first policy term. Policy fees are not charged to you again when your policy is renewed for another policy term.

If your insurance company charges a policy fee, you will not be able to avoid this expense when you start your policy with that company. The best way to avoid additional policy fees is to keep your policy in force, and keep it with the same insurance company for as long as possible.

INSTALLMENT OR BILLING FEE

If you pay for your automobile insurance premiums through an installment plan, such as quarterly or monthly payments, your insurance company may add a fee to each installment. This fee covers the company's administrative costs associated with processing the payments and continuing your policy coverage.

Installment fees vary significantly from company to company. Some automobile insurance companies may charge only a few dollars; others may charge $10 or more for each payment made under an installment plan. A few states limit installment fees to a certain percentage of the total policy premium or otherwise restrict an insurer's ability to charge fees for periodic policy payments.

Some insurance companies will waive installment fees or charge reduced installment fees if you agree to enroll in an Automatic Clearing House

(ACH) payment system. An ACH system automatically debits your checking or savings account for the amount of each premium payment when it becomes due. Insurance companies are willing to reduce or waive fees for policyholders who enroll in an ACH program because it eliminates much of the administrative work associated with processing policy payments and because it makes it much more likely that the insurer will receive valid, on-time payments for each premium installment.

The easiest way to avoid installment fees is to pay your premium in full at the beginning of each policy period. If this is not possible, ask your agent if your insurance company has an ACH program you can use to reduce or eliminate your installment fees.

LATE FEE

If you do not make your policy premium payments by the date shown on your bill, your insurance company may impose a late fee. Late fees vary from company to company — some insurance companies charge as much as $10 or more each time your payment is not received by the premium due date.

Some companies will give you a grace period, such as two or three days after your premium is due, during which they will accept your premium payment without imposing a late fee. A handful of states restrict the ability of insurance companies to impose late fees on automobile insurance policies — for example, Arizona law currently requires insurers to consider payments received up to five days after the premium due date to be timely, so insurance companies cannot impose late fees on policy premium payments made during this period.

Naturally, the best way to avoid late fees is to make sure your premium payments are always received by your insurance company by the due date on your bill. If you have difficulty remembering to mail in premium payments, you may want to consider enrolling in an ACH program if one is offered by your insurer.

NON-SUFFICIENT FUNDS (NSF) FEE

This fee is charged to your policy if the check or other negotiable instrument you use to pay your premiums is returned by your bank, credit union, or other financial institution. A non-sufficient funds fee is charged every time a payment is returned.

Some states limit the amount that an insurance company can charge for a non-sufficient funds fee to the actual expense incurred by the company. For example, in a state with this limitation, if a bank charges an insurance company's account $25 for the presentation of a check that is returned, the insurer would be able to charge you a non-sufficient funds fee of only $25. Other states do not place this limitation on insurers and allow the companies to charge amounts that reasonably cover bank charges and administrative costs associated with a dishonored check or other negotiable instrument.

Of course, the easiest way to avoid incurring a non-sufficient funds fee is to make sure you have the funds in your bank account to cover your premium payments.

Fees can add a significant amount to your policy premiums. You can avoid some of these fees by keeping your policy in force, making payments on time, and paying your entire policy in full. Other fees may be unavoidable, and you should consider these fees when determining your automobile insurance budget.

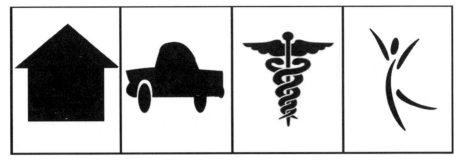

19

AUTOMOBILE INSURANCE FOR HIGH-RISK DRIVERS

─────────

Even the most responsible people sometimes encounter circumstances that make it difficult to obtain insurance in the standard market. Perhaps you have been late for work a few times and been unlucky enough to receive speeding tickets. Maybe you have recently moved out on your own, and you have never had an automobile insurance policy in your name before. Any of these circumstances can put you in the situation of having to seek high-risk automobile coverage.

If you are considered a high-risk driver, you may have difficulty obtaining insurance from a standard agent. However, this does not mean you will have to drive uninsured or apply to your state's assigned risk pool. You may be able to obtain automobile insurance through a specialty company that insures high-risk drivers or through an affiliate company of a standard insurer. This chapter will give you tips on how to obtain insurance at minimal cost if you are designated as a high-risk driver.

WHAT IS A HIGH-RISK DRIVER?

A high-risk driver is a person who has incurred too many violations or had too many automobile accidents to obtain insurance in the standard market. It also includes drivers who have never carried automobile insurance or who have let their automobile insurance lapse or expire without obtaining replacement insurance.

Each insurance company has different criteria that determines who is a high-risk driver. Some companies may consider drivers who have more than a certain number of moving violations, or more than a certain number of rating points for violations to be high-risk drivers. Companies may also place a limit on the number of motor vehicle accidents a driver can have before being placed in a high-risk status.

You may also be high-risk if you have not purchased or maintained your automobile insurance. This often poses a problem for young drivers who have just moved out on their own and who have never purchased an insurance policy before.

Some insurers may place you in the high-risk category based on your credit score. Each state's laws differ with respect to how insurance companies may use credit to determine if you are an acceptable risk, what programs you are eligible for, and how much you will be charged. Still, numerous states allow insurers to place you in a high-risk program or decline to write your policy if you do not meet a certain minimum credit score or if you have a serious negative event such as a bankruptcy or charge-off on your credit report.

Being designated as a high-risk driver does not mean you will always be paying top dollar for your automobile insurance. Once you build a history with an insurance company and your driving record or credit score improves, you may be able to obtain a standard policy with lower premiums. Some companies with both high-risk and standard automobile insurance programs may be able to move you into a standard program at renewal.

HOW CAN A HIGH-RISK DRIVER OBTAIN AUTOMOBILE INSURANCE?

If you are a high-risk driver, there are a number of ways you can still shop for competitive rates on your automobile insurance and find a policy that fits your needs. Here are some of the ways you can easily find an automobile insurance company to insure you at a price you can afford:

- **Ask your agent about a high-risk program.** Many standard automobile insurance companies offer high-risk programs to insure people not eligible for standard auto insurance programs. After you have been insured through a company's high-risk program for a few policy terms, your agent may be able to help you move to a standard program.

- **Search for companies on the Internet to meet your high-risk insurance needs.** You can search Google, MSN, or Yahoo! for terms such as high-risk insurance, nonstandard auto insurance, and minimum-limit car insurance to find a variety of companies that insure high-risk drivers in your state. Many of these companies will allow you to obtain coverage quotes online, and a few will let you purchase your policy online and download a certificate of insurance to print and put in your car.

- **Contact a direct auto insurance writer.** There are several specialty companies that advertise heavily on television and radio stations, seeking drivers with less than perfect driving records or credit scores. These companies offer a toll-free number you can call to speak with a licensed insurance agent — sometimes, these companies staff agents 24 hours a day, so no matter when you call, you can obtain insurance over the phone in less than ten minutes.

WHAT DO HIGH-RISK POLICIES PROVIDE?

In years past, high-risk automobile insurance was associated with bare-bones coverage. Policyholders were limited to only the minimum coverages and limits required by state law. The high-risk market was one that few insurers wanted to pursue, so they provided policyholders with little in the way of coverage and personal service.

Recently, more companies have begun to see the high-risk market as a profitable opportunity to insure people who may otherwise be forced to obtain insurance through an assigned risk pool or drive uninsured. Doing so helps these companies expand their books of business, while providing a valuable service to the driving public.

Today, high-risk automobile insurance policies provide at least the minimum coverages and limits mandated by your state's insurance laws, but they may also offer higher limits on these coverages so that you can purchase additional protection for you and your family.

These policies may also provide comprehensive and collision coverages to pay for damage or loss to your vehicle in the event of an accident, theft, vandalism, or other loss. They may offer high deductibles to help keep your premium costs for these coverages down. Some high-risk insurance companies will not allow you to select comprehensive and collision coverages with a $0 deductible. This also helps reduce the cost of your premiums, because the company will not have to spend a great deal of money adjusting and settling small claims — these costs are passed on to each policyholder in the form of higher rates.

In addition to these coverages, high-risk policies may also offer a variety of optional coverages, such as medical payments, towing and rental coverage, or coverage for optional equipment on your vehicle, such as chrome rims, custom stereo equipment, and aftermarket detailing.

As the high-risk market has become more competitive, the array of coverages and services offered by insurers in this market is beginning to become indistinguishable from those offered under standard policies.

IS HIGH-RISK AUTOMOBILE INSURANCE EXPENSIVE?

High-risk automobile insurance policies often carry higher premiums than comparable standard policies. After all, your insurance company is assuming risks that carry a much higher probability of loss than in the standard market. The company has to charge rates that are high enough to cover its anticipated claims as well as administrative, marketing, and payroll expenses.

You may find, though, that high-risk insurers offer a variety of discounts, sometimes more than those offered by standard companies, which you can use to lower your premiums. For example, claims-free renewal discounts are common among high-risk insurers. Vehicle-related discounts, such as those for air bags, anti-lock brakes, and passive restraints, are also common.

Even if the premiums per policy term are higher than for a comparable standard automobile insurance policy, most high-risk insurers allow policyholders to pay premiums in monthly installment payments. Although you may incur fees for each payment, a monthly payment plan can be a good way to obtain automobile insurance if you are unable to pay for an entire policy term up front.

WHAT IF I NEED AN SR-22?

Many states require drivers to carry an SR-22 for a certain number of years if they have been convicted of certain moving traffic violations or if they have been caught driving without mandatory insurance. An SR-22 is a certificate transmitted from your insurance company to your state's Department of Motor Vehicles or Department of Transportation. This certificate attests that you carry at least the minimum coverages and limits required by your state's insurance laws.

Depending on your state's laws, you may have to carry an SR-22 for three to five years. If you let your insurance coverage lapse or cancel, your insurance company is required to notify the Department of Motor Vehicles or the Department of Transportation that your SR-22 is no longer valid. If this happens, you will be asked to provide a new SR-22 from another insurance company, or your driver's license and vehicle registration may be suspended.

High-risk automobile insurance companies provide SR-22s for many drivers. When you contact an agent or fill out an online quote form, be sure to note that you need an SR-22. After you begin your policy, your insurance company will file the SR-22 with the appropriate state office. You may be charged a fee for this filing; however, you will have to pay this fee only once, unless you let your policy lapse and your insurance company has to file another SR-22 when you reinstate your policy.

No one wants to be considered a high-risk driver. If this has happened to you, though, you can rest easy knowing there are many insurance companies today that are willing to offer you quality coverages at competitive prices.

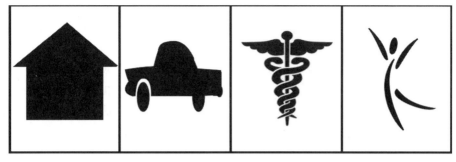

20

WHAT TO DO IF YOU CANNOT OBTAIN AUTOMOBILE INSURANCE

———

As you learned in the last chapter, if you have a large number of traffic violations or accidents on your motor vehicle report or if you have several losses on your CLUE report, you may not be able to obtain insurance through a standard automobile insurance carrier. Most drivers that cannot obtain insurance in the standard market are able to insure their vehicles through a high-risk carrier.

Unfortunately, this is not the case for every driver. Depending on how many violations, accidents, or losses appear on your driver reports, you may find that even high-risk automobile insurance carriers are unwilling to insure you.

If you are unable to obtain automobile insurance by calling agents or shopping for insurance online, you may still be able to insure your vehicles through your state's automobile insurance plan.

Each state has a program designed to provide insurance to people who would not otherwise be insurable. You can obtain information about your state's automobile insurance plan from any insurance agent licensed to write automobile insurance in your state. If an agent is unable to provide you with this information, you can find out how to apply for state coverage by contacting your state's insurance department.

To qualify for your state's automobile insurance plan, you will have to be declined coverage by at least three automobile insurance carriers. If you suspect you will be unable to obtain insurance through the primary insurance market, it is a good idea to ask each insurance agent that is unable to provide coverage for a declination letter. This letter will show the date you applied for coverage, the name of the company that declined to provide you automobile insurance, and the reason the insurance company declined coverage.

The specific coverages available through state automobile insurance plans vary from state to state. You will at least be able to obtain the minimum liability limits required by your state, as well as any other state-mandated coverages. In some cases, you may also obtain comprehensive and collision coverage on your vehicle to financially protect you in case of an accident.

Primary insurers are required to write state automobile insurance plan policies based on their market share (the percentage of automobile insurance policies written relative to all other licensed insurers) in a particular state; however, most states allow insurers to cede, or permit another insurer to write, these policies. State automobile insurance plan policies are written by either primary insurers, or by specialty companies that exist solely to write automobile insurance plan policies.

After you have been insured through your state's automobile insurance plan for a time, typically one year, you may be eligible for a policy through the primary market. Often, you will be able to obtain an automobile insurance policy through the company that provided insurance through the state automobile insurance plan.

State automobile insurance plan policies are quite expensive compared to policies available in the primary market, but if you are unable to obtain insurance elsewhere, this can be a good method for meeting your state's automobile financial responsibility requirements.

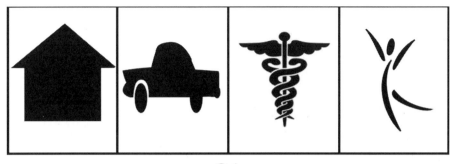

21

HEALTH INSURANCE

We now turn to the topic of health insurance, another type of insurance that is crucial to your family's financial stability. In the next several chapters, you will learn what health insurance is, how you can use health insurance to manage the financial risks that come with illness and injury, and ways you can save money on your health insurance premiums.

WHAT IS HEALTH INSURANCE?

If you have been to the doctor's office or emergency room recently, you know how much basic healthcare can cost. A simple checkup at your doctor's office can cost you $100 or more, and a trip to the emergency room can cost you thousands, even if you come away with just a prescription.

If you have an illness or injury that puts you in the hospital, even for an overnight stay, the costs associated with receiving healthcare can climb even higher. A brief stay in the hospital can cost $10,000 or more, especially if you require intensive care or surgery to address an injury or health condition.

Few of us have the financial reserves to pay for a trip to the emergency room or the hospital. Even routine doctor's office visits or medications can add up to thousands of dollars over the course of a year.

Health insurance can help you to manage your healthcare costs. In exchange for payment of periodic premiums, healthcare coverage will pay part of the costs of your physician visits, prescription medications, emergency room and urgent care services, hospitalizations, and surgeries.

Most health insurers offer several different types of plans with different coverage limits, deductibles, coinsurance requirements, and exclusions. You can choose the type of health insurance coverage you need based on your health, life style, and financial situation.

There are many health insurance plans that also offer disability coverage, which will pay a portion of your earnings in the event that you become ill or injured and are not able to work for a time. The length of this coverage is not as great as disability coverage offered by life insurance policies, but it is important coverage to have in place if you become disabled for more than a month. Health insurance may also cover dental expenses, from routine cleanings to major dental surgery, and vision expenses, such as eye exams and glasses or contact lens purchases.

WHY DO YOU NEED HEALTH INSURANCE?

Many people, especially people without children and professionals just starting in their careers, assume that health insurance is an unnecessary expense. Health insurance premiums, even for employer-sponsored plans, can cost hundreds of dollars per month, and many young people simply feel the burden of these premiums represents too great an expense to justify buying this type of insurance.

The truth is that though health insurance premiums are more expensive than ever, even beginning professionals need this insurance to protect their financial well-being. A single accident or illness can put a working professional at risk of financial disaster — even an outpatient hospital stay for a routine procedure such as an appendectomy can result in a hospital bill of thousands of dollars or more. You cannot assume you will never become sick or injured, no matter how young you are or how well you maintain your health.

Health insurance can also help pay for long-term expenses if you become disabled because of an extended illness or injury. If you were diagnosed with a long-term illness today that prevented you from working for several months, how would you replace your income for the period during which you were unable to work? Unless you have saved up several months' worth of your salary, paying your mortgage and other monthly bills would be a difficult task.

Another reason to purchase health insurance while you are still healthy is once you are diagnosed with an illness, you may not be able to obtain health insurance coverage, or an insurer may be unwilling to pay for treatment and services related to your condition. You cannot wait until you need health insurance to purchase a policy.

If you decide to have children, some health insurance policies will cover the costs of prenatal care, such as obstetrician's office visits, ultrasounds, and other measures necessary to ensure the good health of your unborn child. It will cover the costs of delivery and postnatal care services after your child is born. Your child will also be added to the policy at birth, so any healthcare necessary to address congenital health problems would be covered under your health insurance policy as well.

An excellent reason to buy health insurance is it will give you the financial incentive to consult a doctor or specialist before an illness or health condition becomes severe enough to require major medical treatment of hospitalization. Many people are more likely to see a doctor for a routine checkup, a nagging pain, or other symptom if they have health insurance in place to pay for the office visit. This allows your doctor to help you detect and treat conditions early, which can save you thousands of dollars in avoided medical expenses and lost work time.

The best reason to purchase health insurance is it helps you manage the financial uncertainty of your current or future medical needs. You may be in perfect health today, but the unfortunate reality is you could be diagnosed with an illness tomorrow that would require long-term medication, frequent doctor's office visits, hospitalization, or surgery. Not having health insurance in place before you become ill or injured can be an efficient path to financial disaster.

Understanding your health insurance options is important because knowing the types of insurance available will help you choose the type of plan that is right for you.

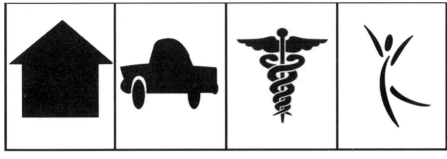

22

TYPES OF HEALTH INSURANCE POLICIES

Although coverages under health insurance plans vary by company, there are four basic types of health insurance you can purchase to protect your financial well-being.

SINGLE INDIVIDUAL HEALTH INSURANCE

Single individual health insurance is a policy that covers only you. This type of health coverage includes provisions for paying for routine medical expenses and prescription costs, as well as incidental medical expenses such as emergency room treatment, urgent care services, hospitalization costs, and surgeries. Your policy may also include benefits for preventative care, vision, and dental costs, depending on the plan selected by you or your employer.

The cost of a single individual health insurance policy is a small fraction of the cost of family medical coverage. If you do not have a spouse or dependant, this can be a good option for obtaining health insurance at a relatively affordable premium.

If you experience a qualifying event, such as marriage or the birth of a child, you will be able to convert your health insurance policy to a family plan by notifying the insurer of the qualifying event. You must do so within 30 days of the event — otherwise, the health insurance company is not obligated to allow you to convert your policy to a family plan.

FAMILY HEALTH INSURANCE

Family health insurance plans offer the same coverage as single individual health plans but cover other members of your immediate family. If you are married and have children, this is the most affordable way to obtain health insurance for your family.

If you are married but do not have children, you may choose to insure yourself and your spouse under a family health insurance plan, or you and your spouse may each elect to be covered under separate individual health insurance plans. Often, the cost of two individual plans is lower than the cost of one family health plan. If you and your spouse have a child later, you can compare the costs of a family plan through your respective health insurance plans and decide which policy to convert to a family plan.

Family health insurance plan premiums do not ordinarily change depending on the number of children you have. You will pay the same monthly premium for a family plan whether you have one child or six children.

SUPPLEMENTAL HEALTH INSURANCE

Supplemental health insurance is designed to cover costs associated with illness or injury that are not covered by your primary health insurance policy. It is important to understand that if you become ill or injured, prescription drug costs and hospital charges are not the only costs you will incur. Here are some of the most popular types of supplemental health insurance coverages available today:

- **Accidental Death and Dismemberment Coverage.** This type of policy is designed to provide payment for medical services not covered by your primary health insurer in the event of an accident. It also pays a stated benefit to your beneficiaries if you die as a result of an accident and to you if you become permanently disabled because of an accident. If you lose a limb or digit, you may be entitled to a portion of the death benefit listed in your policy.

- **Specific Disease Coverage.** This policy will directly pay you a set amount if you are diagnosed with a covered disease. This amount may be paid on a lump sum or a per-day basis and is independent of any medical expenses you may incur for treatment of the disease. You are free to spend the money however you want.

  Common diseases covered under specific disease coverage policies include cancer, leukemia, multiple sclerosis, and renal disease. The benefit amount may be different for each disease covered under this type of policy.

- **Hospital Indemnity Insurance.** This supplemental policy pays you a specified amount for each day you are hospitalized, up to a maximum number of days specified in your policy. The benefits under a hospital indemnity policy are not reduced by any coverage for hospital or medical expenses paid by your primary health insurer.

This is a valuable coverage, because if you are hospitalized, you will incur additional living expenses above the cost of your hospital stay and medical treatment. You may need to pay someone to care for your children or pick them up from school, shop for groceries for your children, mow your lawn, or handle other household tasks you would perform if not for your hospitalization. Hospital indemnity insurance is inexpensive but can provide needed funds to cover your additional living expenses if you are hospitalized.

- **Excess Medical or Catastrophic Medical Coverage.** This policy protects you from being required to pay hospital and medical expenses that exceed the policy limits of your primary health insurance plan, or medical expenses not covered by your primary plan. Excess medical coverage carries a high deductible — you or your primary health insurer may be responsible for $20,000 or more of your hospital or medical expenses before coverage begins under this type of policy.

  If you have sufficient financial reserves to cover the deductible, excess medical coverage can be a good solution for obtaining inexpensive healthcare coverage to pay for catastrophic medical expenses; however, most people who purchase this type of policy use it as a supplement to primary health coverage.

- **Dental and Vision Coverage.** Some primary health insurance policies offer benefits for dental or vision services, but there are a number of plans under which these coverages are not available. You can purchase these coverages under a supplemental policy to cover the costs of dental procedures and vision-related expenses.

  Dental coverage pays for preventative care expenses, such as periodic dental checkups, x-rays, and routine cleanings. It also provides benefits for corrective dental work, such as root canals, fillings, bridge work, and oral surgery. It may also pay a portion of your expenses for dentures and orthodontic work, although coverage for orthodontics has decreased in recent years. Dental coverage will not pay for cosmetic dental work, such as tooth whitening.

Vision coverage pays for routine vision exams and screenings and pays a portion of the costs of corrective lenses, eyeglass frames, and contact lenses. Some vision plans pay for a portion of your expenses for contact lenses ordered by mail. Insurance companies may limit you to a specified list of vision care providers and may pay a reduced benefit or refuse to pay for vision services if you use a provider outside the insurer's network.

Dental and vision coverage is sometimes offered on a reimbursement basis — if this is the case, you will have to pay for the costs of dental or vision services, and then the insurance company will send you a check for the benefit amount.

• **Long-term Care Coverage** pays for medical, nursing, and therapeutic expenses if you become partially or completely disabled as a result of a disease, illness, or accident and require care on a long-term basis. These services are not covered under a primary health insurance policy, so long-term care coverage can be valuable. Services may be provided on an inpatient or outpatient basis — many times, you can receive all of your long-term care at home.

Long-term care coverage benefits are paid on a per-day basis — you can obtain coverage that will pay from $40 to more than $200 per day for medical and nursing services.

Your policy may stipulate that an elimination period must be met before coverage can begin — an elimination period is a specified number of days that you must receive and pay for long-term care expenses out of pocket. Be sure to check the length of the elimination period before you purchase a long-term care policy. An elimination period of 60 days may mean you will be responsible for $10,000 or more of your long-term care expenses before your benefits begin.

TRAVEL INSURANCE

If you are traveling outside the United States, medical facilities in foreign countries may not honor the coverage provided by your primary health policy. If you require medical attention while traveling in a foreign country, you may be required to bear the entire cost of the care you receive.

Travel insurance is a special policy that provides medical coverage while you are in another country. These are short-term policies that cover time periods from five days to one year and provide benefits for illnesses, accidents, and medical emergencies. It may also provide limited coverage for an acute onset of illness caused by a pre-existing condition.

Some travel insurance policies also offer additional coverages, such as benefits for accidental death while traveling abroad, repatriation expenses, and the costs of medical evacuation.

This is an important policy to purchase if you will be traveling outside the United States or living in another country for a short time. If you currently have a primary health insurance policy, you will not need to submit to a medical exam to obtain this coverage.

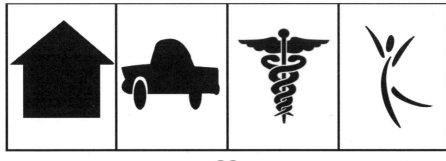

23

MEDICARE & MEDICAID COVERAGE

This chapter will describe two federally sponsored healthcare programs in the United States: Medicare and Medicaid. You will learn the eligibility requirements for each type of coverage, as well as the types of care that are covered and the limitations of each program. Understanding Medicare and Medicaid is essential if you are considering either type of coverage as an alternative to standard healthcare insurance.

Many people do not understand Medicare or Medicaid and assume that one of these health coverage plans will automatically cover their healthcare expenses in the event of an illness or an accident. However, this is often not the case. Each plan has strict eligibility requirements, so they do not automatically cover healthcare costs you are unable to pay.

MEDICARE

Medicare is a federally sponsored health coverage program that is available to most senior citizens in the United States and people living in the United States who have permanent total disabilities. Certain parts of this coverage are provided at no cost to eligible people.

Eligibility

To qualify for Medicare coverage, one of the following must apply to you:

- You are over the age of 65.

- You are under the age of 65 but are permanently disabled and have been receiving Social Security disability benefits for at least two years.

- You are in need of a kidney transplant or are undergoing continuing kidney dialysis.

- You have been diagnosed with Amyotrophic Lateral Sclerosis (ALS or Lou Gehrig's Disease).

In addition, you must be a United States citizen or have been a legal resident of the United States for at least five years.

Coverages

The schedule of coverages available under Medicare is divided into four parts. The coverages under each part are as follows:

Part A — Hospital Insurance

Part A of Medicare coverage provides inpatient hospital benefits with a $992 deductible per benefit period. For the purpose of this coverage part, a benefit period is defined as beginning the day the patient is admitted to the hospital and ending 60 days after the patient is discharged or otherwise leaves the hospital.

Medicare Part A provides coverage for a hospital stay of up to 150 days per benefit period. The patient is responsible for coinsurance requirements for hospital stays of 61 days or more:

- For days 61 to 90, the patient is responsible for a coinsurance payment of $248 per day.

- For days 91 to 150, the patient is responsible for a coinsurance payment of $496 per day.

Medicare Part A also pays for treatment received at a skilled nursing facility. There are no deductible requirements, but the patient is required to pay a $124 per day coinsurance requirement for any skilled nursing care after 20 days. Medicare does not provide any benefits for skilled nursing care after 100 days.

Hospice care is also covered under Medicare Part A. There is a co-payment of $5 for outpatient drugs and a 5 percent coinsurance requirement for respite care services.

There is no coverage available for home healthcare under Part A.

Part B — Medical Insurance

Part B of Medicare coverage is designed to pay for home healthcare, doctor's office visits, and outpatient hospital services that are not covered by Part A.

It also pays for laboratory tests, such as blood work and X-rays; preventative screenings, such as flu shots, mammograms, bone mass measurements, cardiovascular screenings, prostate cancer tests, and diabetes screenings.

Ambulance services, mental healthcare, and outpatient therapy are also covered under Medicare Part B. This coverage will cover one physical exam administered within six months of the date the patient enrolls in Part B.

Part B is considered an enhanced coverage part; thus, it is not provided on a no-cost basis. In 2007, the monthly premium for Part B coverage is $93.50 for most Americans who meet the eligibility requirements. Premiums are significantly higher for individuals with gross incomes higher than $80,000 and married couples with gross incomes of $160,000 or more. For these higher-income individuals, Medicare Part B premiums are based on modified adjusted gross income and can range between $106 and $161.40 per month.

Medicare Part B coverage is subject to an annual deductible of $131. Most services covered under this part are also subject to a 20 percent coinsurance requirement. If a doctor does not accept the Medicare Part B assignment, you may subject to an additional co-payment amount up to 15 percent of the medical costs incurred. Acceptance of an assignment means the physician has agreed to accept Medicare's predetermined fee as payment in full for services provided.

Part C — Medicare Advantage

Part C offers coverages available under Parts A and B under private health insurance plans and may also offer prescription coverage available under Part D. Part C does not offer any additional healthcare benefits above those offered through the other coverage parts.

Part D — Prescription Coverage

In 2006, Medicare Part D was added to cover the costs of prescription drugs. There is an additional premium of $27.35 for this coverage part, which is offered through Medicare approved private health insurance plans. The list of formulary drugs covered varies among the plans, as do deductibles and co-payment requirements. Medicare coverage pays benefits for medical care and services administered only within the United States.

There are a number of costs and services that are not covered by Medicare. For example, Medicare does not cover long-term care administered in the home or in a nursing care facility. It also does not cover the costs of eye exams, corrective lenses, dental care, or hearing aids.

Enrolling in Medicare

If you are already receiving Social Security benefits when you turn 65 years of age, you will automatically be enrolled in Medicare parts A and B. You may choose to decline Part B, but if you choose to enroll in this coverage part later, you may incur a late enrollment fee. You will not automatically be enrolled in Medicare Parts C or D — you will need to enroll in these coverage parts through a Medicare-approved private health insurance plan.

If you are not already receiving Social Security benefits when you turn

65, you will need to enroll in Medicare — you will not automatically be enrolled on your 65th birthday. You can apply for Medicare Parts A and B at any Social security office during your initial enrollment period, which begins three months before you turn 65 and ends three months after your 65th birthday.

If you do not enroll in Medicare Parts A and B during your initial enrollment period, you may apply during a yearly enrollment period, which runs from January 1 through March 31 of each year. Your coverage will begin on July 1 of the year in which you enrolled in these coverage parts. If you do not apply for these Medicare coverage parts during your initial enrollment period, you will incur a penalty for each year after you turned 65 in which you did not enroll — the penalty will be added to your Part B premiums.

If you are applying for Medicare benefits because of a total permanent disability, you need to visit your local Social Security office for an application.

MEDICAID

Medicaid is a no-cost health insurance plan for individuals who are below certain income levels and who have a permanent disability or otherwise meet one of the eligibility groups designated by the state government. Your assets will also be considered when determining whether you are eligible for Medicaid coverage.

Because Medicaid is a state-sponsored plan, the maximum income levels and eligibility groups vary by state. You can visit your state's Social Security Administration office to learn about the eligibility requirements for people in your state.

Medicaid coverage has three primary components:

- Health insurance coverage for low-income individuals and people with certain disabilities.

- Long-term care for elderly people and individuals with disabilities.

- Supplemental health coverage for individuals enrolled in Medicare, to pay for healthcare expenses not covered under Medicare.

Because of the restrictive nature of Medicaid plans, most people treat Medicaid as a last resort. Only people who are unable to afford any type of health insurance through the primary market and those people who are uninsurable should consider coverage under this plan.

Both the Medicare and Medicaid plans have restrictive eligibility requirements and offer limited coverages. If you qualify for either of these plans and do not feel additional health insurance coverage is necessary, you may wish to pursue coverage under Medicare or Medicaid.

For most working people, though, these plans are not feasible, because they are either unavailable or do not provide sufficient benefits to meet a working family's needs. If either of these plans were available on the open market, it is unlikely many people would enroll.

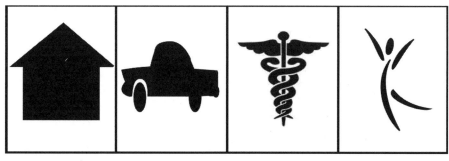

24

MANAGED CARE PLANS

Many health insurance policies available in the United States today are based on managed care plans. In a managed care plan, the health insurer controls several aspects of your healthcare that you may not be aware of when obtaining healthcare services.

For example, a health insurer offering coverage under a managed care plan has already negotiated rates for services with certain medical professionals. It will pay healthcare providers less than you would pay out of pocket for the same services if you visited the healthcare professional with no insurance.

Managed care plans allow health insurance companies to control the costs associated with claims, billing, and other administrative services. This, in turn, helps keep your premiums as low as possible.

This chapter will describe the major types of managed care plans and distinguish the differences among each one.

HEALTH MAINTENANCE ORGANIZATIONS (HMOS)

In the 1970s, United States federal law passed legislation that required all companies with more than 25 employees to offer an HMO alternative if another type of health insurance plan was offered.

An HMO is an insurance entity that establishes contracts with hospitals, doctors, specialists, and other medical professionals and organizations to obtain healthcare services for its subscribers at a fixed cost per member. This helps control healthcare costs and can be beneficial to healthcare professionals who contract with an HMO, because they are able to establish a captive client base through the HMO.

HMOs focus on reducing the costs of healthcare in several ways:

- They establish measures to reduce the number of unnecessary hospital admissions among subscribers.

- They emphasize preventative care, including diagnostic screenings and routine medical exams, as a means of minimizing the financial effects of serious illness or disease.

- They focus on medical care that will help minimize the number of days a member spends in the hospital.

- They implement measures to reduce administrative costs associated with providing healthcare benefits to their members.

An HMO operates under one of three models to achieve its objective of providing healthcare benefits at minimal cost:

GROUP PRACTICE MODEL

A group practice model resembles a clinic operation, because under this model, a group of specialists and physicians practice healthcare in a single medical facility. The facility may choose to provide medical services only to HMO members, or it may provide services to patients who are not HMO members at a higher cost. If the facility provides healthcare services only to HMO members, then the physicians and specialists are salaried employees of the HMO.

Under the group practice model, you can receive healthcare without having to go outside the facility, unless hospitalization is required. Referrals are made internally, allowing you access to various specialists in the same facility. If a particular specialist is not available within the group practice, the HMO may establish a special contract with an outside specialist to provide medical services. The HMO also establishes contracts with hospitals to provide healthcare services not available within the facility, in the event hospitalization is required.

STAFF MODEL

The staff model HMO system differs from the group practice model in that the HMO owns and operates the medical care facility. It may build the facility, staff it with physicians and specialists, and manage its day-to-day operations. The doctors and specialists working in the facility are employees of the HMO.

Like the group practice model, an HMO establishing a medical care facility under the staff model may choose to provide services only to its plan members.

INDEPENDENT PRACTICE ASSOCIATION MODEL

Physicians and specialists who contract with an HMO under the independent practice association model are not employees of the HMO, nor do they work in a facility owned or operated by the HMO. Instead, physicians and specialists under this model may work in their own practices or may be employed by a hospital or other facility.

Under this model, subscribers receive a list of approved physicians operating within a geographic area, including physicians practicing within a wide variety of specialty disciplines. As a member under this model, you would choose a doctor as your primary care physician and visit the doctor for treatment. If the primary care physician is unable to treat you, then he or she would refer you to a specialist within the independent practice association. These specialists may be employed by hospitals or other medical facilities that have contracted with the HMO.

The independent association model is the most common form of HMO and the form that insures most people who subscribe through an employer-sponsored group health insurance plan.

ADVANTAGES AND DISADVANTAGES OF HMOS

Like any type of insurance plan, there are several advantages and disadvantages of selecting an HMO for your health insurance needs. Before selecting an HMO, take the time to consider how important these factors are to you.

Advantages

- Copayments are low for healthcare services and prescriptions. There is often no co-payment requirement for prescription drugs, and copayments for office visits are $10 or less. Compared to other types of plans, this advantage can save you a significant amount of money if you have to visit your primary care physician or a specialist.

- Premium costs can be lower for coverage through an HMO plan than for other types of plans, because HMOs take aggressive steps to control claims and administrative costs.

- You will have access to a number of preventative care resources. HMOs place a significant emphasis on preventative care as a means of keeping subscribers healthy and reducing claims costs. Whether you are interested in quitting smoking or losing weight, concerned about a disease or condition that runs in your family, or want to receive checkups to maintain your health, HMOs will provide benefits for these services.

- You can be reasonably certain you will not lose your coverage under an HMO. An HMO is prohibited by law from terminating your coverage for any reason other than fraud or material misrepresentation, nonpayment of premiums or copayments, failure to continue to meet eligibility requirements, termination of the group contract under which you obtained coverage, or your violation of your contract terms.

Disadvantages

- You will always have to consult your primary care physician when seeking care for a medical condition and will have to rely on your primary care physician to refer you to an appropriate specialist in the HMO network.

- HMOs do not provide coverage for healthcare services performed outside your designated geographic service area, except for emergency services.

- In some cases, an HMO's focus on cutting costs may compromise the quality of care you receive. In recent years, HMOs have used administrators, rather than physicians, to make decisions regarding the delivery of care within the HMO. Also, HMOs have been criticized for providing bonuses and incentives to doctors for conserving medical resources.

PREFERRED PROVIDER ORGANIZATIONS (PPOS)

In contrast to HMOs, PPOs do not use primary care physicians as gatekeepers to control the healthcare received by members. Instead, PPOs manage costs by increasing the level of benefits available to members when they choose to use the services of a physician, specialist, or hospital within the PPO's network.

For example, if you needed to see a gastroenterologist, your PPO plan may require a $75 co-payment if you receive care from a gastroenterologist outside the PPO's preferred provider network but may require only a $20 co-payment if you use a gastroenterologist within the network.

This financial incentive is a PPO's primary means of cutting costs. A PPO does not require you to use doctors and facilities within the network, and it does not require you to obtain a referral from your primary care physician before visiting a specialist outside the network.

PPO plans involve a yearly deductible that must be met before payment for healthcare services will begin and a coinsurance requirement after your deductible is met. Your deductible is a flat dollar amount, such as $500 or $1,000, which you must pay out of pocket each year. Your coinsurance requirement is expressed as a percentage of the healthcare costs you incur after your deductible has been met.

You may have several deductible and coinsurance choices available through your PPO plan. If you and your family will use the PPO network often, it may be cost effective to select a high deductible, such as $1,000, and a low coinsurance requirement, such as 10 percent, so that your PPO plan will pay 90 percent of your healthcare costs after you meet your deductible. If you are not sure how much you will use your PPO's network, it may be more cost efficient to select a lower deductible, such as $250, and a higher coinsurance requirement, such as 30 percent, so you have a better chance of getting some use out of your PPO plan.

ADVANTAGES AND DISADVANTAGES OF PPOS

Advantages

- There is no need to consult a primary care physician for a referral to a specialist. PPOs do not use primary care physicians as gatekeepers to manage costs.

- You are not restricted to doctors, specialists, and hospitals within a network or geographic service area. You are free to choose any medical professional or facility with which you feel comfortable.

- If you have already established a relationship with a physician or specialist, a PPO plan will allow you to continue receiving healthcare services from that medical professional.

Disadvantages

- PPOs can be significantly more expensive than HMOs. In addition to copayments, you may also be required to pay a yearly deductible and a coinsurance requirement for healthcare costs that exceed your yearly deductible.

- Benefits for preventative care may not be as readily available as they are through an HMO. You may have to pay for smoking cessation classes or weight-loss training on your own if you are a member of a PPO.

- If you do not exceed your yearly deductible, you will not receive any type of benefit from your PPO plan, because your benefits will not begin until after you have paid your yearly deductible.

Choosing between an HMO plan and a PPO plan can be difficult, especially if you are not able to reasonably anticipate your healthcare needs. If you do not mind being restricted to certain doctors and certain geographic areas, an HMO may adequately meet your needs. If you are willing to pay more for your coverage in the form of deductibles and copayments to have the freedom to visit healthcare professionals outside a network, a PPO may be right for you.

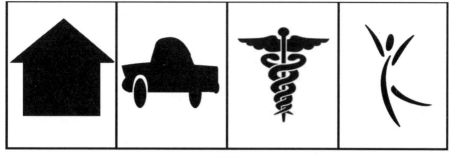

25

SELECTING AN EMPLOYER-SPONSORED HEALTH INSURANCE PLAN

If you work for an business with at least 25 employees, your employer may sponsor a group health insurance plan. An employer purchases a master policy from a health insurance company, and employees who enroll in the plan are supplied with certificates of insurance as proof of health insurance coverage.

Group health insurance plans offer several advantages over insurance plans available to individuals:

- Your employer may subsidize a portion of the insurance premiums. Few employees are fortunate enough to work for a company that pays for 100 percent of its employees' health insurance premiums, but many employers pay for a portion of employees' insurance as a benefit of working for that employer. This can help make group health insurance coverage more affordable than individual health insurance plans not sponsored by an employer.

- Premiums for group health insurance plans are determined by experience rating. The health insurance company issuing the master policy to the employer takes into account the claims made by all of the subscribing employees and establishes premiums in anticipation of the number and dollar amount of claims the health insurer anticipates for the next plan year.

  Experience rating offers a significant potential for cost savings over individual health insurance plans, which base rates on community rating — a formula that takes into account the average costs for various healthcare services charged by various providers in a geographic area.

- You can obtain coverage through a group health insurance plan without a physical exam. When you begin employment with a company that offers a group health plan, you will have the opportunity to enroll in the plan simply by electing to do so within the time specified by your employer.

- If you have been insured under a group health plan immediately before beginning a new job, your new employer's group health plan may have a shorter waiting period for coverage for pre-existing conditions or may not be permitted to impose a waiting period for pre-existing conditions. This offers a significant advantage over individual health insurance plans, which are not obligated to cover pre-existing conditions without a significant waiting period.

- You will often obtain better coverage though a group insurance plan than through an individual insurance plan. Because the health insurer providing a master policy to an employer has the benefit of experience rating, an employer can often afford to offer coverages through the insurer's policy that would be cost prohibitive under an individual policy.

- Because your employer wants to continue to provide health insurance to employees at the lowest premium possible, it may actively seek to reduce claims costs to maintain the best possible coverage at the lowest cost. Employers often institute wellness programs to help employees live healthier life styles and may be willing to pay for some on-site preventative care, such as flu shots and smoking cessation programs.

- Your group health insurance premiums can be paid on a pre-tax basis. Your employer can deduct your portion of the premium payments from your paycheck before any taxes are applied to your gross income. This can save you several hundred dollars a year over purchasing a healthcare policy on a post-tax basis.

The main drawback of choosing to obtain group health insurance through your employer is the lack of choice of your coverages or premiums. Health insurers providing group health coverage to a company's employees may revise premiums, coverages, deductibles, or entire plans each year, and you may have little say about how these changes affect you. Still, many Americans find the cost savings obtained by choosing a group health plan far outweighs the lack of choice in coverages or premiums.

TYPES OF EMPLOYER HEALTH PLANS

Primary group health insurance plans offered by employers fall into one of two categories: PPOs and HMOs. These plans were discussed in detail in Chapter 24.

Another plan that may be available through your employer is a cafeteria plan. Cafeteria plans allow you to pick and choose from a variety of medical services and pay for these services on a pre-tax basis. The money you contribute can be paid toward medical, wellness, and other expenses, such as:

- Premiums for group health insurance policies.

- Deductibles, copayments, coinsurance requirements, and other medical expenses not paid for by your primary health insurance policy.

- Alternative medicine not paid for by your primary health insurance policy, such as chiropractic services, acupuncture and acupressure treatments, aromatherapy, *reiki*, and massage therapy.

- Smoking cessation and weight-loss programs (these may be covered under an HMO but may not be covered under a PPO).

- Contraceptives, including birth control pills.

- Alcoholism treatment and counseling.

- Psychiatric and psychological counseling and treatment.

- Day care for your dependents.

Your employer may offer a number of other coverages as part of your group health insurance plan or as separate plans that comprise part of your employee benefits package. These coverages may include dental and vision coverage, short-term and long-term disability, and accidental death and dismemberment.

ENROLLING IN YOUR EMPLOYER'S PLAN

When you begin employment with a company that offers a group health insurance plan, you will have the option of joining the plan. Some companies specify a minimum period of employment, such as 60 or 90 days, before an employee is eligible for health benefits. This is because the company bears numerous administration cost associated with adding a new employee to the group health insurance plan, and it does not want to incur these costs for employees who may join the company and quickly leave.

If you do not join your employer's health insurance plan at the initial enrollment period, you will have to wait until the employer's next regular enrollment period, which may occur near the end of each calendar year. Again, your employer may allow employees to join the plan or modify coverage selections during specified periods to minimize the costs associated with managing the health insurance plan.

If you have joined your employer's group health insurance plan and experience a qualifying life-changing event, such as marriage, divorce, death of a covered family member, birth of a child, or your spouse's loss of health insurance coverage, you will be able to make changes to your health insurance policy regardless of whether you are within a regular enrollment period. You need to notify your company of the qualifying event within 30 days of the date it occurred. If a child has been adopted or born into your family, coverage will begin on the date of adoption or birth of the child.

You will not be subject to a physical exam when enrolling in your employer's group health plan.

WHAT TO DO IF YOU AND YOUR SPOUSE BOTH HAVE GROUP PLANS AVAILABLE

If you and your spouse both work for employers that offer group health insurance plans, you will be faced with choosing which plan to use to provide coverage for your family's healthcare needs. There are a number of factors you will need to consider when deciding whether to choose health insurance coverage through your own employer or through your spouse's employer:

- **The types of health insurance plans available.** You or your spouse may be eligible for a health insurance plan that is set up as a Preferred Provider Organization (PPO), a Health Maintenance Organization (HMO), a cafeteria plan, or another type of plan. Evaluate your family's healthcare needs to determine which of the plans available through your respective employers will best meet your family's needs.

- **The premium costs associated with each plan.** As noted earlier in this chapter, an employer may elect to pay a portion of employees' health insurance premiums. Plans through different companies may carry different premiums depending on the experience rating for that company's members. These factors can result in significantly different premium costs, even if your employer and your spouse's employer offer the same type of plan.

- **The likelihood that you or your spouse will change jobs or become self-employed.** If you or your spouse carry the health insurance coverage for your family and change employers, you will be able to subscribe to your new company's health insurance plan, assuming a plan is available through your new employer. However, you will find you have to deal with new premiums, different coverages, and perhaps a different type of health insurance plan. If you have already established a primary care physician and have established relationships with specialists or doctors employed by a specific hospital, you may find that a new health insurance plan will not cover services provided by some of these medical professionals or will cover their services only on an out-of-network basis.

  If the member of your family who carries the group health insurance policy becomes self-employed, you may see a drastic increase in premiums. Health insurance for self-employed individuals is often more costly than group health insurance coverage — these policies are rated differently than group policies, and you will not have an employer to pick up part of the premium costs. Also, if your family switches to a self-employed individual health insurance policy, your new insurer may not cover pre-existing conditions for up to one year after you begin coverage.

It is important that you take the time to carefully evaluate each plan available and your family's unique needs. Once you select a plan, you will not be able to switch your family to a different plan unless you are within your annual enrollment period, you or your spouse leave your employer, or some other qualifying event occurs.

The next chapter covers COBRA, a federal plan that will help you maintain your healthcare coverage if you separate from your employer and do not have coverage available through your spouse's employer.

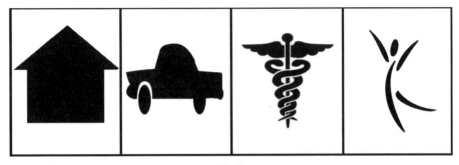

26

COBRA — KEEPING YOUR HEALTH INSURANCE IF YOU LOSE YOUR JOB

As long as you are employed by a company that offers a group health plan, you will likely be able to obtain the health insurance you need to protect your family's health and personal finances. If you part ways with your employer, though, one of the first things you may wonder about is whether you will be able to continue to provide health insurance for your family while you are looking for a new job.

Thanks to the Consolidated Omnibus Budget Reconciliation Act (COBRA) of 1986, you have the option of keeping your health insurance for a time under most circumstances. This act gave individuals employed with a company offering a group health plan and enrolled in that plan the ability to continue coverage under the same policy for at least 18 months after parting ways with the company. Its provisions apply not only to the policyholder, but also to any other family members covered under the policy at the time the policyholder parted ways with his or her employer.

Coverage under COBRA also applies to any newborns that are born while COBRA protection is in effect. You must inform the insurer continuing your health insurance coverage of the newborn within 30 days of birth.

Your rights under COBRA apply regardless of whether you are laid off, fired, or leave the company of your own volition. The exception is if you are terminated for gross misconduct, in which case you will have no benefits protection under COBRA.

The provisions of COBRA are designed to give you time to find another employer and become enrolled in that employer's group health plan or obtain health insurance through some other means, such as an individual health coverage policy.

HOW MUCH WILL IT COST?

Under the provisions of COBRA, your health insurance company cannot charge you more than 102 percent of the premiums charged while you were employed with the company sponsoring the health insurance plan.

This does not necessarily mean the amount you pay will be only 2 percent higher than when you were employed with the company. There are two reasons for this. First, your employer may have been subsidizing part of your premiums while you were employed with that company. Once you part ways, your employer is under no obligation to continue subsidizing your health insurance premiums. Second, while you were employed with the sponsoring company, you were paying for your portion of your health insurance premiums with pre-tax dollars. After leaving your employer, you will have to pay the full amount of your premiums as if you were using post-tax money.

COVERAGE FOR PRE-EXISTING CONDITIONS

An advantage of continuing your coverage under COBRA is that when you do obtain new health coverage through another employer, you will be able to demonstrate the health insurance coverage necessary to waive the new health insurer's waiting periods for pre-existing conditions. As long as you are able to prove coverage for a period equal to the elimination period (typically one year), the new health insurer will not be able to use that period to deny claims related to the pre-existing condition. This is an important consideration, particularly if you or a covered family member have chronic or long-term health problems that require ongoing treatment.

Although you will likely be paying more for the same health insurance benefits than you were while you were employed, obtaining coverage under COBRA is less expensive than purchasing an individual health insurance policy and continues to protect your family's health and financial security while you are securing employment and new health insurance coverage with another company.

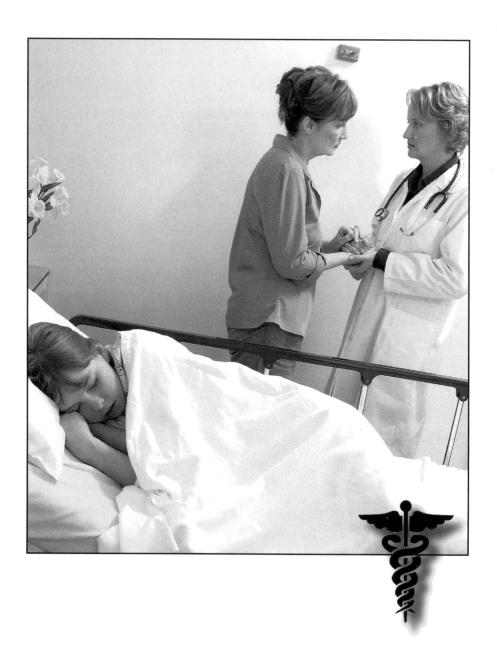

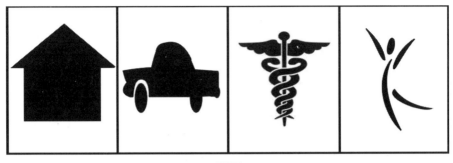

27

HEALTH INSURANCE BENEFITS FOR THE SELF-EMPLOYED

Obtaining affordable health insurance is a fairly simple process for most people who are employed by companies that offer group health plans. If you are an entrepreneur, though, you will find the process of obtaining health insurance at a price you can live with a little more challenging.

The fear of not being able to obtain health insurance is the number one reason people cite for deciding not to start a business. You may have heard of business owners who decided to work part time at a retail job to have access to affordable health insurance benefits. Other entrepreneurs rely on their spouses' employers to provide health insurance at reasonable rates, but if their spouses became unemployed for a long time, their families could be in significant financial trouble.

Fortunately, there are a few ways you can obtain health insurance for your family if you decide to go into business for yourself. This chapter will give you some ideas for finding coverage at a price you can live with while you are building your own business.

USE COBRA AS LONG AS POSSIBLE

In Chapter 26, you learned about the protections available under COBRA. As noted in that chapter, your premiums are not likely to be as low as when you were employed with the company, but it is still less expensive than purchasing an individual health insurance policy, and it will require the least attention while you are getting your business off the ground.

As long as you were not fired for gross misconduct, you can keep the same policy under COBRA for at least 18 months. You will undoubtedly have other stress in your life and other things competing for your attention in the early months of your business, so this can be a good way to make sure your family's health is covered until you can devote more time to searching for a replacement policy.

LOOK FOR TRADE GROUPS OR GUILDS

If your COBRA coverage is about to expire, or you have a little extra time to explore other options, you may be able to find a group health insurance policy through a guild or group dedicated to providing services to people in your field of business. Restaurateurs, artists, writers, retailers, and many other types of entrepreneurial professionals have guilds and groups to help them obtain services and items they could not effectively obtain individually — including group health insurance.

Many people think group health insurance policies are available to only employers and their employees, but many guilds and professional groups are able to negotiate group insurance policies for their members. Of course, they will not pay part of your health insurance premiums like an employer, but you will be able to obtain coverage at a lower premium rate than if you purchased an individual health insurance policy.

Another advantage of enrolling in a group health policy through a guild or group is a group health insurer cannot deny you coverage because of a pre-existing condition. Any amount of time you were covered through your previous employer or through COBRA will also apply toward any elimination periods imposed by the guild's group health insurance plan.

A quick search on a major search engine such as Google, MSN Search, or Yahoo! will give you the Web sites of any trade groups or guilds for people in your particular field. The Web sites will tell you how you can obtain brochures on the guilds' group health insurance plans or provide links to health insurers' Web Sites where you can learn more about the coverages and premiums for the group plans.

You will need to pay a yearly membership fee for the privilege of belonging to a trade group or guild, but this membership fee is modest. For example, if you are a writer, you can join the National Writer's Union at **www.nwu. org** for as little as $120 per year. The savings you will obtain by enrolling in the National Writer's Union's group health insurance plan will more than offset the cost of membership — plus, you will have access to all of the other services this organization offers to working writers.

FIND AN INDIVIDUAL HEALTH POLICY

If your coverage under COBRA has expired and you are unable to obtain a group health insurance policy through a trade guild or group, you may still be able to obtain an individual health insurance policy.

Individual health insurance policies provide the same types of coverages as group health policies. You may find policies designed as HMO or PPO plans, and some of these plans may include coverage for vision, dental, and other services. These plans primarily differ from group health insurance plans in three ways:

- **Premium cost.** Because individual health insurance plans are rated based on community rating, rather than experience rating, your premiums for an individual health insurance plan may be much higher than premiums for a comparable group health insurance plan. Community rating means the health insurer takes into account the predominant costs for services charged by medical professionals and healthcare facilities in your area. The health insurer cannot base premiums on experience, because it cannot pool a group of members to share risks — the insurer's ability to realize a profit from writing and maintaining your policy rests on the number and amount of claims submitted by you and your family.

- **Coverage limits, deductibles, and coinsurance.** Individual health insurance policies may offer high deductibles and coinsurance requirements and lower policy limits, in an effort to keep premiums affordable. You will find that many individual health insurance plans will offer policies with yearly deductibles of $2,000, $5,000 or more and coinsurance requirements of 20 to 30 percent. This means if you carry individual heath insurance, you may still have to pay a large amount out of pocket for your healthcare services.

- **Underwriting and acceptability criteria.** Individual health insurance plans are not subject to the same restrictions as group health insurance plans, so you may be denied coverage for an individual policy if you have a history of disease or other ongoing health condition. If you are accepted for coverage, an individual health insurer may choose to impose a waiting period for any pre-exiting conditions, and you will not be able to use prior coverage to fulfill the waiting period requirements like you could with a group policy.

Individual health insurance policies tend to offer less coverage for higher premiums than group health insurance policies. Still, if you do not have another option, this type of policy can help protect you from major medical expenses if you or a family member is hospitalized or requires surgery.

HEALTH SAVINGS ACCOUNTS (HSAS)

As long as you and your family are insurable under an individual health insurance policy, another option that may be financially beneficial to you is to purchase and maintain an HSA.

When most people refer to an HSA, they mean a high-deductible health insurance plan coupled with a savings account that resembles an Individual Retirement Account (IRA). In this section, HSA will be used to refer to the medical savings account component of your plan.

The annual deductible for your health insurance policy can range from $1,000 to $5,250 for individuals, and from $2,000 to about $10,000 for families — the higher the deductible, the lower your monthly premium costs will be.

Although the health insurance portion of your plan carries a high deductible, certain expenses can be covered by an HSA-qualified plan outside the yearly deductible. When HSAs were established, the United States Congress was concerned that, because of the high deductible of these plans, people would hesitate to seek routine checkups, medical exams, and preventative care. The following services are paid for by the health insurance portion of your HSA, without regard to your annual deductible (although coinsurance requirements may apply):

- Routine physical exams and checkups.

- Immunizations for child and adult patients.

- Diagnostic screenings, such as mammograms.

- Smoking and tobacco cessation programs.

- Weight-loss and obesity programs.

- Prenatal and child wellness care.

- Other preventative care services.

You can contribute up to $5,250 per year to your HSA and use the money to cover medical expenses that are not covered by the health insurance portion of your plan. You will receive a 100 percent tax deduction for the money you place in your HSA each year, so you are essentially putting away this money tax free. Also, the money you withdraw from the plan to pay for qualifying medical expenses will not be subject to taxes or penalties, so you can cover your medical expenses with tax-free dollars.

Any money you contribute to your HSA during a calendar year that is not used to cover medical expenses will be carried over to the next plan year. You can continue to save money in your HSA for future medical expenses or use the plan to save for retirement.

Withdraws made for nonmedical expenses after you turn 65 would be subject to income tax but not withdrawal penalties; withdrawals for nonmedical expenses made before you turn 65 are subject to a 10 percent penalty plus applicable income taxes. Withdrawals for medical expenses are not subject to taxes or penalties regardless of your age at the time of withdrawal.

The money you place in your HSA will earn interest comparable to an IRA or 401(k) plan, so you can use an HSA as both a medical savings tool and an investment vehicle.

Let us look at an example of how you can invest through your HSA and still have the money available to withdraw tax free if the funds are needed to pay for medical expenses not covered by your health insurance plan: Suppose you contribute $5,250 to your HSA every year for 30 years. If you do not need the money to pay for medical expenses, the money you contribute will continue to gain interest as long as it is held in the HSA. Let us suppose the money you have placed in your HSA gains interest at a rate of 8 percent per year. At the end of 30 years, you would have more than $680,000 available for retirement or medical expenses.

An HSA can be a good choice if you are self-employed, want to keep you health insurance premium costs low, and need to save money for retirement.

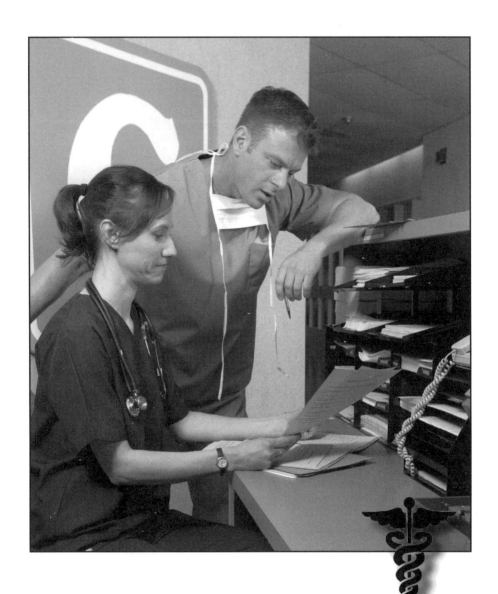

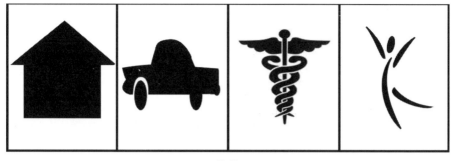

28

LIFE INSURANCE

So far, this book has covered ways you can obtain insurance as protection for your family's home, personal automobiles, and health. Now, you will learn how to obtain affordable insurance to protect your family's finances if you died or became disabled due to an accident or severe illness.

WHAT IS LIFE INSURANCE?

No matter how well you manage your personal risks, there is always the chance you will die or become permanently disabled. It is an unfortunate fact of life no one wants to think about, but to financially protect your family, it is crucial you have life insurance protection in place to help your family continue to meet its financial obligations if you passed away or became unable to work.

Life insurance pays your family a lump sum, subject to the policy limits you select, if you pass away during the time covered by the insurance policy. If you select disability coverage, it will also make periodic payments if you become disabled and are unable to work, so you can continue to pay your bills and provide for your family's financial needs.

WHY WOULD YOU NEED LIFE INSURANCE?

Many people, especially young people starting out on their own, feel that life insurance is not a necessity. As long as you are young and healthy, the possibility of dying or becoming disabled seems like a distant event. Unfortunately, any person can die in a car accident, while on the job, or due to an accident in his or her home. Although the probability of such an event may be low, the financial consequences your family would face in the event of your premature death would be quite serious.

Do you own your home? If you currently make mortgage payments on your home, you likely contribute some, if not all, of the income necessary to make your monthly mortgage payments. Without money to continue making these payments, your house would go into foreclosure, and your surviving family members would be forced out of their home.

Do you carry balances on your credit cards? It is a mistake to assume your credit card debt would be erased in the event of your death. Your creditors will look to your spouse and other resident family members for payment of your credit card balances if you die. If the money to make these payments is not available, your family could be forced into bankruptcy.

Even if your mortgage has been paid off and you have no credit card or other unsecured debt, your family has become accustomed to the life style that your income helps to provide. Life insurance can help your surviving family members maintain that life style without having to sacrifice because of your early passing.

Your family would also be responsible for your funeral and burial expenses, which can reach $15,000 or more in some parts of the United States. Even if you choose to be cremated, your family will incur considerable expense in cremation services and a remembrance ceremony.

Let us now suppose you were involved in an accident in which you did not die but were permanently incapacitated and unable to return to any kind of work. In this case, all of your income would disappear, but in addition to being responsible for your contribution to the mortgage, debt, and life style of your household, your family members would also be responsible for additional services and items needed to care for you.

Life insurance is a necessity because no one is guaranteed another day of life, but financial obligations remain after you die. To protect your family's financial well-being in the event of your death or permanent disability, you need to have an appropriate life insurance plan in place to take care of your family's expenses.

Let us now move on to several of the most common types of life insurance available so you can begin choosing a policy that best fits the needs of you and your family.

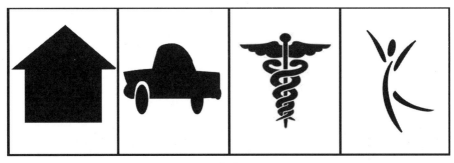

29

TYPES OF LIFE INSURANCE POLICIES

This chapter will describe the types of life insurance policies available and give you the information you need to decide which type of life insurance policy is right for you. Life insurance can be a confusing topic because there are many types of policies available to help you meet your specific financial objectives.

TERM LIFE INSURANCE

The most common type of life insurance available is term insurance. This type of insurance allows you to select the number of years you wish to be insured and pays a lump sum to your family if you die during the period in which your life insurance policy is in force.

Term life insurance represents one of the most affordable options for obtaining life insurance, because it pays only if you die during the policy term. Life insurance companies use actuarial statistics to determine the probability that it will have to pay under your policy — the less likely the company will have to pay, the lower your premiums will be for coverage.

There are relatively few factors used to determine your policy premiums:

- **Your age.** Your term life insurance premiums are partially based on your age when you start coverage under the policy. Insurance companies may use your actual age or may round up to the next age if you are within six months of your next birthday. The younger you are when you begin your policy, the lower your premiums.

- **Your gender.** Statistically, insurance companies have a higher probability of paying out on a life insurance policy for a male than for a female. Accordingly, life insurance rates for males tend to be higher than those for females.

- **Your weight.** No one likes to tell how much they weigh, but if you are applying for a life insurance policy, you will have to disclose your weight on your application. Overweight individuals may be rated higher than average or slim individuals, or they may be placed in a different life insurance program designed to handle higher risks.

- **Your tobacco use.** If you smoke or use tobacco in any other form, you are more likely to die during the policy term than if your are a nonsmoker. Premiums for smokers and other tobacco users are substantially higher than for non-tobacco users for this reason. If you are currently a nonsmoker, insurance companies may ask if you have used tobacco in the past — if you have not used tobacco in any form in the year before you purchased your policy, your company may allow you to be rated as a nonsmoker. Note, though, that the insurance company may require you to submit to urine or blood tests to verify the absence of tobacco in your bloodstream.

- **The state in which you live.** Premium rates differ for each state, depending on the insurer's claims experience in each state. This may be based on the availability of quality healthcare, the presence of environmental toxins, the life style of residents, or other factors unique to a state.

- **The length of the policy term.** Insurance companies know they are more likely to pay out on policies with 30-year terms than policies with 10-year terms, particularly for younger policyholders. If you purchase a term life insurance policy when you are 35 years old, you will pay a higher premium for a 30-year term policy than for a 10-year policy.

- **The face value of the policy.** The larger your life insurance policy, the higher your premiums will be. Life insurance rates are expressed as a premium cost per $1,000 of coverage, so if you take out a $200,000 policy, you will pay ten times as much for insurance premiums than if you had taken out a $20,000 policy.

Types of Term Life Insurance Policies

There are two primary types of term life insurance — level term and decreasing term.

A level term policy allows you to keep the same amount of coverage throughout the life of the policy. If you take out a $20,000 level term policy, your policy will pay $20,000 on your death, regardless of whether you die the day after coverage begins or the day before it ends.

You can choose either a level term policy with annual renewable terms, which keeps your benefit amount the same but raises your premium every year, or a level term policy with a level premium term, which keeps both your benefit amount and your premium payments the same over the life of the policy. Annual renewable terms are better if you want to pay less for your coverage while you are younger and then increase your payments as your age and income increase. If you do not want to worry about rising life insurance premium costs every year, a level premium policy is a better option.

A decreasing term policy allows you to keep your premium payments the same each year but decreases the amount of the benefit each year. If the primary purpose of buying a term life policy is to cover an expense such as a mortgage or installment loan, this can be a good choice — as the balance on your mortgage or loan decreases, the benefit amount on your policy decreases as well. Decreasing term policies are less expensive than comparable level premium term policies.

Why Choose Term Life Insurance?

Term life insurance is a good choice for people who want to keep their premium costs low while providing their families with a means for financial security during a particular time. This type of policy is primarily used for meeting short-term objectives, rather than for building a nest egg that can be passed on to children, grandchildren, or other beneficiaries.

For example, suppose Joe Smith is a middle manager at an accounting firm. He is 35 years old and has two small children, ages 3 and 5. He owns a $200,000 home with 20 years remaining on the mortgage and has an additional $10,000 in unsecured debt.

Assuming Joe and his wife do not plan on having any more children, a 20-year term insurance policy may be a good choice for Joe, for a couple of reasons. First, if he lives through the end of the policy, he will have paid off his mortgage at the time the policy expires. Second, when the policy expires, his children will be out of the house and may have graduated from college with undergraduate degrees.

In 20 years, Joe's financial situation will be much different than it is today. He will no longer have to manage a mortgage payment, and his children will have begun careers of their own. He and his family will need less money to maintain their life style. Thus, the end of Joe's term life insurance policy will coincide with a sharp reduction in the money needed by Joe's family to live.

If Joe dies within the policy term, his term life insurance policy will help his family take care of a number of expenses that have not yet disappeared, such as his monthly mortgage payment, his credit card debt, and the living, educational, and other expenses of his two children.

Another reason to purchase term life insurance is because you can convert most term policies to a whole life policy at any time before the policy expiration without a physical exam. If you do decide to convert the policy to a whole life policy, you will pay premiums based on your age at the time of conversion instead of at the time you purchased your policy. Still, this can be a good way to protect your family with inexpensive coverage and keep your options open to buy a different type of policy as your needs and your financial situation changes.

Disadvantages of Term Life Insurance

The main disadvantage of a term life insurance policy is that, like automobile insurance, if you do not use the coverage while the policy is in force, you will never get any of your premiums back. Term insurance does not pay you any part of your premiums or the face value of the policy if you outlive the policy term.

Another disadvantage of a term life insurance policy is if you get to the end of your policy term and find your financial plan has not gone as expected — say you had to refinance your mortgage or had another child unexpectedly — you will not be able to extend coverage under your policy at the same policy premiums.

In Joe's case, if he was unable to pay off his mortgage in 20 years, or he and his wife had another child, he would have to purchase another life insurance policy at the expiration of his 20-year term policy. Unfortunately, he will be rated as a 55-year-old rather than a 35 year old, so his premiums will be substantially higher for the new policy.

The third disadvantage of term insurance is there may not be any provision for disability. Term life is an all-or-nothing coverage — either you die during the policy period and use the benefit, or you outlive the policy and lose all of your premiums.

WHOLE LIFE INSURANCE

In contrast to term life insurance policies, whole life policies do not expire on a stated date or pay nothing if the insured outlives the policy. Instead, whole life insurance is designed to provide life insurance protection for the policyholder's entire life and allow the policyholder to build cash value within the policy to lower premium payments or provide funds for financial emergencies in later years.

When you purchase a whole life policy, your premiums are calculated based on your age at inception and are ordinarily calculated on the assumption you will continue to pay premiums until you reach age 100. This means your premiums never change for as long as you own your policy.

If you do not wish to continue paying premiums until you reach age 100, you can select a limited payment or single premium whole life policy.

A limited payment whole life policy shortens your premium payment schedule so you can make all of your payments by a certain age. This helps ensure you will not be using your retirement money to pay your life insurance premiums. For example, you could select a whole life policy with a "Life Paid Up at 65 (LP65)" clause that requires you to make all of your premium payments by the time you are 65 years old. Of course, this means you will be adding 35 years worth of premiums to the amount you will be paying between now and the time you turn 65, so your premium payments will be much higher than with a standard whole life policy. If you take out this type of policy when you are 30 years old, and your yearly premiums are $500, a LP65 clause would double your premium payments:

Premium per year of life insurance coverage: $500

Total premiums (all years): $35,000

Number of years you would pay on a standard whole life policy: 70

Number of years you would pay under a LP65 clause: 35

Total payment per year under a LP65 clause: $35,000/35 years = $1,000

A single premium whole life policy requires you pay the entire premium for all years of coverage at inception. Using the above example, this means you would have one premium payment of $35,000, and your policy would be paid up to age 100. Your insurance company may be willing to offer you a discount if you are able to purchase a single premium whole life policy.

As you continue to pay premiums on a whole life policy, you will build cash value within the policy. Cash value is money in your life insurance policy that you can use to pay premiums in later years or borrow against if you need money for expenses. You can also allow the cash value in your policy continue to accumulate.

If you live to age 100, your whole life policy will pay you the face value of the policy or the cash value accumulated within the policy, whichever is more. This money is yours to do with as you please.

If you die before you reach age 100, the policy will pay your beneficiaries the face amount of the policy, less any negative cash value that has occurred because of loans or withdrawals against the policy or unpaid premium payments.

Whole life policies often also include a benefit if you become permanently disabled. At the minimum, they may continue to pay your premiums if you become disabled, so you can continue your life insurance coverage. Some whole life policies have riders that will pay a certain amount, maybe half the amount of the death benefit, if you suffer a permanent disability. Other policies contain disability riders that will pay a portion of the monthly salary you earned while you were able to work. These riders will cost you additional premium but are worth the cost if you are injured in an accident or develop an illness that prevents you from working.

Why Choose Whole Life Insurance?

If you want to build a cash amount future generations can use to pay for college, living expenses, or to start their own nest egg, whole life allows you to do this while protecting your family in the short term as well.

Whole life policies also allow you to build cash value with your premium payments, unlike term life insurance policies, which never build any cash value. You can borrow against the cash value of your whole life policy or use it to make future premium payments.

Regardless of whether you die during the policy term, your policy will pay out. Your policy will either pay your beneficiaries when you die, or pay you when you reach age 100. Some people prefer this over term life insurance, which will not pay out unless you die during the policy term.

Disadvantages of Whole Life Insurance

The primary disadvantage of whole life policies is they are substantially more expensive than comparable term insurance policies. You may pay two to three times the amount that you would pay for the same coverage under a term insurance policy.

An adage that has surfaced in recent decades is: "Buy term and invest the difference," which means, because term insurance is so much cheaper than whole life, you are better off taking the extra money you would have spent on a whole life policy and placing it in an investment vehicle that would allow your money to grow more quickly. Whether this is sound advice is largely a matter of personal preference, but it is a worthwhile consideration, particularly if a life insurance agent is trying to push you toward a whole life policy.

The other disadvantage of whole life insurance is, unless you have the ability to pay for your policy all at once or through a limited pay plan such as a LP65 plan, you will continue making premium payments into retirement and beyond. It is important to consider carefully whether you want the obligation of making policy premium payments when you are no longer working and are living on retirement savings or Social Security income.

UNIVERSAL LIFE POLICIES

If you are concerned your financial position may change as you grow older and you may not be able to make life insurance premium payments, another option for purchasing life insurance is a flexible premium policy.

The primary type of flexible premium policy offered in the United States is the universal life policy. Universal life is a type of modified whole life insurance that allows the policyholder to modify the death benefit of the policy and adjust how much he or she will pay for premiums.

Here is how a universal life insurance policy works: When you make your premium payments for a universal life policy, the insurance company will deduct administrative expenses from your payments and place the remainder into a cash value account. The amount necessary to keep your death benefit in force is then deducted from this cash value account. If you pay more than the minimum amount necessary to keep your death benefit in force, your policy will build cash value.

Your insurance company will provide you with a table showing the minimum amount you need to pay to keep your death benefit in force and how additional amounts will allow you to build cash value within your policy.

Universal life insurance allows you to treat cash value within the policy as an investment, because it pays interest on the cash value in your policy. This consists of two parts — the minimum guaranteed interest rate and the excess interest rate.

Your insurance company will state a minimum guaranteed interest rate that will be credited to the cash value in your policy. This guaranteed rate is around 4 percent per year.

Excess interest is the amount of interest over the guaranteed minimum the insurer plans to earn for a calendar year. If the company plans to earn 7 percent for a given year, then your excess interest would be 3 percent, bringing the total interest credited to your cash value to 7 percent for that year. Excess interest is guaranteed for one year and may change from year to year, depending on the company's profits.

Why Purchase Universal Life Insurance?

Universal life insurance gives you the ability to protect your family from financial disaster in the event of your death, while giving investment-minded people the opportunity to build a substantial cash value within the policy.

It also gives you the ability to adjust your premium payments according to your budget. If you encounter a time in your life when you need money for other things, such as emergency home repairs, a replacement automobile, or your child's college tuition, you can elect to pay the minimum amount necessary to keep your death benefit on your universal life policy in force. You can use the cash value you have already built up in your universal life policy to make the minimum premium payments.

Another advantage is your ability to take out loans against the cash value in your policy to pay for unexpected expenses.

Disadvantages of Universal Life Policies

As with whole life policies, universal life policies are substantially more expensive than term policies with similar death benefits. Although you may make lower minimum premium payments to keep your death benefit in force, if you choose to do this, you will not be building any cash value in your policy and will not be able to take advantage of the interest applied to the cash value. Essentially, if you are going to be able to make only the minimum premium payments, you are essentially purchasing an expensive term policy with a term that ends when you turn 100 years old.

VARIABLE UNIVERSAL LIFE POLICIES

Variable universal life policies are similar to traditional life insurance policies in many respects, with one important difference: Instead of having your insurance company decide the interest rate you will earn on the cash value in your policy, you can place the cash value into a number of separate accounts that operate in a manner similar to mutual funds. The money in your cash value account can also be invested in stocks or bonds.

Variable universal life policies give you a greater opportunity for investment growth, because you will be able to direct the cash value of your policy to the investments of your choice. It is important to note, however, that variable universal life policies do not guarantee a minimum interest rate, so you have the potential for loss as well as the potential for gain.

Equity indexed universal life policies are a fairly recent addition to life insurance offerings. These policies work the same as other types of variable universal life policies, except you have the ability to invest your cash value in index options that follow the movement of an index such as the Dow Jones Industrial Average or the S&P 500.

IMPAIRED RISK POLICIES

Although there is no assigned risk pool or state FAIR plan to help you obtain life insurance if you cannot find coverage in the standard market, a number of life insurance companies offer impaired risk plans, which can help you obtain life insurance under most circumstances.

Impaired risk policies have more lenient underwriting criteria than standard policies, so insurance companies that offer these policies can accept applicants with a variety of diseases and conditions, such at diabetes, cerebral palsy, heart conditions, high cholesterol, and hypertension.

If you have more than one significant health condition, though, you may have difficulty obtaining insurance even through an impaired risk policy. Cerebral palsy coupled with a heart condition, for example, may disqualify you from coverage.

The premium rates for impaired risk policies are significantly higher than for standard or preferred risk policies. Also, a company offering an impaired risk policy may place a maximum on the amount of coverage you are able to obtain. Often, this maximum is not enough to pay off your mortgage or other large expenses, but it may provide some coverage to take care of funeral and burial expenses, pay off unsecured loans, and provide limited funds for your family while they are making life style adjustments as a result of your death.

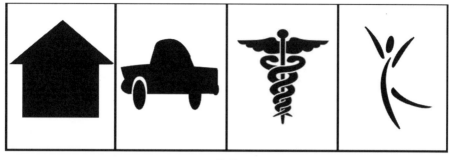

30

WAYS TO SAVE MONEY ON LIFE INSURANCE

Now let us explore some of the ways you can save money on your life insurance premiums. The ability to reduce your premiums will allow you to buy more insurance to provide additional protection for your family, save money in investments and savings accounts, and enhance your family's life style.

GROUP LIFE INSURANCE POLICIES

If you are employed with a company that offers a benefits package, your employer may offer you a group life insurance policy at little cost to you. Many companies offer this benefit for free, particularly if an employee enrolls in the company's group health insurance plan.

If your employer offers you free life insurance coverage that will protect your family in the event of your death, you can use this protection in addition to any life insurance you purchase to provide additional funds for your family to pay off your mortgage, settle credit card debts, take care of your funeral and burial expenses, or pay for any other expenses they may not otherwise be able to manage.

Group life insurance policies provided through many employers will also provide death benefits for your spouse, so if your spouse dies while you are employed with the company, the group policy will pay you a lump sum to cover expenses your spouse left behind.

You will be eligible for benefits under your employer's group life insurance policy only for as long as you are employed with that company. Once you leave your employer, any coverage you had through your employer's group life insurance plan will be terminated — unlike group health coverage, you will not be able to take your life insurance coverage with you. Still, it can be a way to obtain temporary life insurance coverage at little or no cost.

DECLINING CHILD LIFE INSURANCE

When you purchase a life insurance policy through an agent, your agent may try to convince you to insure the lives of your dependent children. At first, this seems like a good idea — insuring your children protects you from financial loss that would result if they would pass away before reaching adulthood.

In reality, child life insurance is more of an emotional decision than a rational one. If your child passed away, you would undoubtedly be overwhelmed with grief, but would you incur any financial loss outside the funeral and burial expenses for your child?

Unless your child is actively earning a substantial income — say your child is a well-known movie actor, catalog model, or commercial actor

— the death of your child will have far more emotional consequences than financial ones. For most Americans, purchasing any child life insurance outside benefits for funeral and burial expenses is a waste of premium dollars that could be put to better use elsewhere.

The exception is when your child has a health condition that you believe would prevent him or her from obtaining a traditional life insurance policy on reaching adulthood. Some child life insurance policies can be converted to traditional policies once the child reaches the age of majority — many times, without the need for a physical exam. If you believe your child will have difficulty being accepted for a life insurance policy on reaching adulthood, it may be wise to purchase a child life policy to give him or her the opportunity to obtain a level of life insurance protection when he or she leaves your home.

TAKE CARE OF YOUR HEALTH

Because life insurance rates are partially based on your health factors, including whether you use tobacco or are overweight, taking care of your health is an important way to keep your life insurance premiums at a minimum.

If you smoke or use tobacco, find a way to stop. You may not see an immediate decrease in your life insurance premiums, but after you have been tobacco free for a year or more, you may be able to be re-rated as a nonsmoker or find another life insurance policy that will rate you as a nonsmoker. On average, you can save between 15 and 25 percent on your life insurance premiums by qualifying for nonsmoker status.

If you are overweight, make an effort to slim down. Find out the height-to-weight ratio your life insurance company uses to determine whether you are rated as a preferred, standard, or nonstandard risk, and commit to losing weight until you reach the height-to-weight ratio necessary to qualify for your insurance company's preferred rates.

If you have a health condition such as diabetes or asthma, make sure you are taking the appropriate steps to control your condition. Many life insurance companies will look more favorably on an applicant or policyholder who is effectively managing a health condition than one who has taken no steps to control his or her illness. Not only will you feel better, but you may be able to qualify for a lower life insurance rate.

OTHER WAYS TO SAVE ON LIFE INSURANCE

Here are some other ways you can save money on your life insurance premiums:

- **Find out how much your family will need to cover expenses.** It is as easy to overstate your family's financial needs as it is to understate them. Take the time to analyze how much your family will need to cover bills, funeral and burial expenses, and other household expenses. Once you have determined your family's needs, purchase only the amount of life insurance needed to cover those expenses.

- **Look for life insurance through a mutual insurance company that pays dividends to its policyholders.** If a mutual company makes a profit during a given calendar year, it will pay money to its policyholders in the form of dividends. Dividends may be paid in cash, as a reduction in your required premium payments, or as the option to purchase paid-up additions to increase the death benefit of your policy.

Dividends cannot be guaranteed by an insurance company — it would be illegal for a company to do so. However, a mutual life insurance company should be able to provide you with a history of dividends paid to policyholders so you can assess whether the company will pay you dividends that you can use to offset or reduce your insurance premiums.

- **Shop around on the Internet for life insurance rates.** You can find many Web sites that will give you quotes on life insurance policies, and several Web sites will provide you with quotes from multiple companies so you can compare coverages and premiums.

- **Check with the insurance company that provides your automobile or homeowner's coverage to see if you can obtain a discount on a life insurance policy.** Many companies offer multiline discounts and may be able to help you save money on all of your policies if you purchase more than one type.

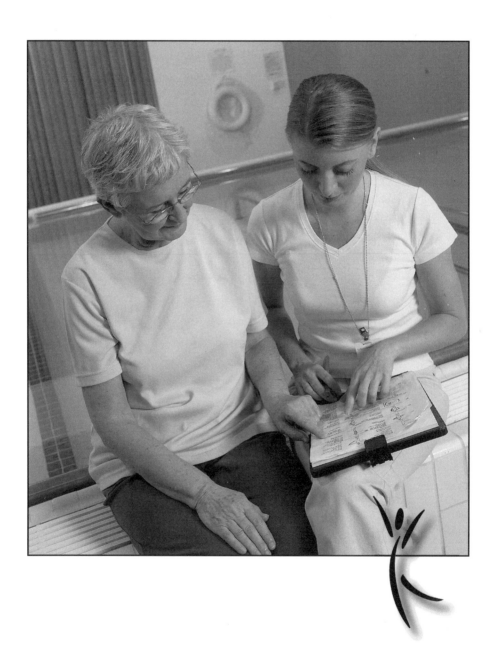

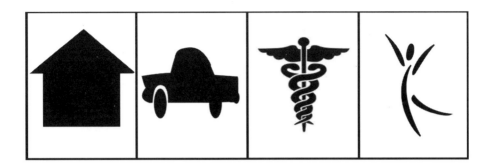

CONCLUSION

Throughout this book, you have been given a wealth of information about the major types of personal insurance necessary to protect you and your family from financial disaster. Certainly, there is more information contained in this book than could be easily digested in a single reading.

Now that you have read through the entire book, keep it with your other important reference materials. As your personal and financial circumstances change, you should refer to parts of this book each time you are called on to make an insurance-related decision for yourself or your family.

Each time you refer to a section of this book, you will become armed with the knowledge and savvy necessary to make sound insurance decisions that will have minimal impact on your budget. You will be able to ask your agent educated questions to make sure he or she is giving you all of the information you need to obtain the best insurance coverage at the best rate. You will also know which types of insurance to avoid because they would provide unnecessary or duplicate coverage, and which types of insurance you and your family cannot do without.

The remainder of this book is divided into four sections to help you quickly find information you will need when you are gathering insurance quotes and deciding which coverages to purchase.

Appendix A provides Web site links to each Department of Insurance in the United States. You can visit these Web sites to find specific information about the insurance laws in your state. You can also review information about individual insurance companies and groups, including their financial strength, the number of years they have been in business, they types of insurance they write, and the number of complaints the Department of Insurance has received concerning their practices and claims-handling ability.

Appendix B contains a glossary of commonly used insurance terms. This reference is divided into sections for terms related to homeowner's, automobile, health, and life insurance, so you can quickly search for terms used by your insurance company or agent when searching for coverage.

Appendix C contains a number of miscellaneous resources you can use to further educate yourself so you can make informed insurance decisions.

Appendix D contains a number or Case Studies of real people who have found ways to save money on auto insurance. Agents and consumers both have participated in these Case Studies, and they provide an enlightening look into the intricate process of saving money on homeowner's, automobile, health, and life insurance.

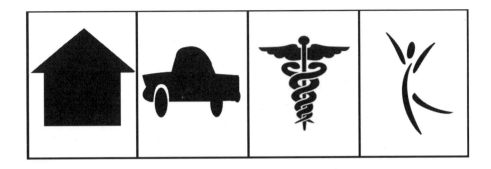

APPENDIX A:
LINKS TO YOUR
STATE INSURANCE
DEPARTMENT WEB SITE

Alabama Department of Insurance:
www.aldoi.gov

Alaska Division of Insurance:
www.dced.state.ak.us/insurance

Arizona Department of Insurance:
www.id.state.az.us

Arkansas Department of Insurance:
www.state.ar.us/insurance

California Department of Insurance:
www.insurance.ca.gov

Colorado Division of Insurance:
www.dora.state.co.us/insurance

Connecticut Web Site:
www.ct.gov
Note: *Connecticut does not currently have a Web site dedicated to insurance topics.*

Delaware Department of Insurance:
http://delawareinsurance.gov

District of Columbia Department of Insurance, Securities and Banking:
http://disr.dc.gov/disr/site/default.asp

Florida Office of Insurance Regulation:
www.floir.com

Georgia Office of the Insurance and Fire Safety Commissioner:
www.gainsurance.org

Hawaii Department of Commerce & Consumer Affairs:
www.hawaii.gov/dcca/areas/ins

Idaho Department of Insurance:
www.doi.idaho.gov

Illinois Division of Insurance:
www.idfpr.com/DOI/Default2.asp

Indiana Department of Insurance:
www.ai.org/idoi/index.html

Iowa Insurance Division:
www.iid.state.ia.us

Kansas Insurance Department:
www.ksinsurance.org

Kentucky Office of Insurance:
http://doi.ppr.ky.gov/kentucky

Louisiana Department of Insurance:
www.ldi.la.gov

Maine Bureau of Insurance:
www.maine.gov/pfr/insurance

Maryland Insurance Administration:
www.mdinsurance.state.md.us/sa/jsp/Mia.jsp

Massachusetts site:
Note: *Go to* **www.mass.gov** *and search for insurance.*

Michigan Office of Financial and Insurance Services:
www.michigan.gov/dleg/0,1607,7-154-10555---,00.html

Minnesota Department of Commerce:
www.state.mn.us/portal/mn/jsp/home.do?agency=Commerce

Mississippi Department of Insurance:
www.doi.state.ms.us

Missouri Insurance Department:
www.insurance.mo.gov

Montana Department of Insurance — State Auditor's Office:
www.sao.state.mt.us

Nebraska Department of Insurance:
www.doi.ne.gov

Nevada Division of Insurance:
http://doi.state.nv.us

New Hampshire Insurance Department:
www.nh.gov/insurance

New Jersey Department of Banking and Insurance:
www.state.nj.us/dobi/index.html

New Mexico Insurance Division:
www.nmprc.state.nm.us/id.htm

New York Insurance Department:
www.ins.state.ny.us

North Carolina Department of Insurance:
www.ncdoi.com

North Dakota Insurance Department:
www.nd.gov/ndins

Ohio Department of Insurance:
www.ohioinsurance.gov

Oklahoma Insurance Department:
www.oid.state.ok.us

Oregon Insurance Division:
www.cbs.state.or.us/external/ins/index.html

Pennsylvania Insurance Department:
www.ins.state.pa.us/ins/site/default.asp

Rhode Island Department of Business Regulation
www.dbr.state.ri.us

South Carolina Department of Insurance:
www.doi.sc.gov

South Dakota Division of Insurance:
www.state.sd.us/drr2/reg/insurance

Tennessee Department of Commerce and Insurance:
www.state.tn.us/commerce/insurance/index.html

Texas Department of Insurance:
www.tdi.state.tx.us

Utah Insurance Department:
www.insurance.utah.gov

Vermont Department of Banking, Insurance, Securities and Health Care Administration:
www.bishca.state.vt.us

Virginia Bureau of Insurance:
www.scc.virginia.gov/division/boi/index.htm

Washington Office of the Insurance Commissioner:
www.insurance.wa.gov

West Virginia Offices of the Insurance Commissioner:
www.wvinsurance.gov

Wisconsin Office of the Commissioner of Insurance:
http://oci.wi.gov

Wyoming Insurance Department:
http://insurance.state.wy.us

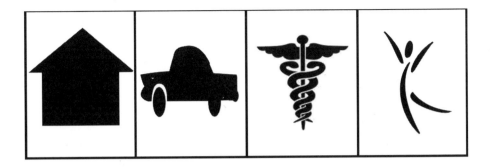

APPENDIX B: GLOSSARY

HOME INSURANCE TERMINOLOGY

Now that you have learned about the features and coverages of the different types of home insurance and the different policy portions, let us take some time to define some of the terms you may encounter while shopping for home insurance.

Actual Cash Value: The depreciated value of an item, as determined by an insurance company, paid to replace an item that is damaged or stolen as a result of a covered loss. Actual cash value does not provide payment for the cost of the item if it were purchased new; rather, it determines the value of the item when the loss occurred. If you owned an item for several years before the damage or theft, actual cash value may not provide a payment sufficient to purchase a replacement item.

Additional Living Expenses: Additional benefits that can be paid to a policyholder when the policyholder's home has been made unlivable due to a disaster, damage, or loss, and temporary housing is required while the home is being repaired or rebuilt. Additional living expenses cover expenses only that the policyholder would not have incurred if not for the damage to the home, such as rent for temporary housing, meals purchased at restaurants because of the lack of cooking facilities in the temporary housing, and additional transportation expenses necessary to commute from temporary housing to work.

Adjusters: Insurance professionals who evaluate the damage caused by a theft, vandalism, or disaster; investigate the circumstances under which damage or a loss to your property occurred; and approve and issue claim payments for valid covered losses. Adjusters may be employees of an insurance company, or they may be independent adjusters who evaluate and investigate losses for a number of insurance companies.

Appraisal: The evaluation of the value of a home or personal property conducted to determine the replacement cost of the property and to determine if the property is eligible to be insured. Appraisal values are based on what it would cost to replace the property in the area where it is located, so values for similar properties may vary from region to region.

Arbitration: A negotiation that occurs when an insurance company and an insured person disagree on the value of a loss or the amount of a claim payment. When arbitration occurs, the parties agree to settle the claim dispute by bringing in a third party to make the final decision. Insurance contracts may mandate the decision of the third party is binding, meaning the insurance company and the claimant must accept a decision made by the third party.

Arson: An act that occurs when a home, insured building, or property is deliberately set on fire. Under common law, arson is considered a felony. Arson can be difficult to prove unless an impartial witness is willing to testify the fire was started deliberately, or evidence is introduced that demonstrates the fire was not started by accidental means.

Beach and Windstorm Plans: State-sponsored programs that allow homeowners to be covered for damage caused by windstorms in areas considered high-risk. Since these areas are prone to damage from these hazards, insurance companies do not want to assume the risk and may elect to refuse coverage. Currently, these plans are offered in Alabama, Florida, Louisiana, Mississippi, North Carolina, South Carolina, and Texas.

Binder: A written or oral agreement that coverage is approved by the agent or insurance company and is extended before the actual policy begins. This allows a policyholder to obtain immediate coverage before the initial premium payment has been made. Coverage for claims made during the binder period is dependent on the initial premium payment being remitted to the insurance company.

Burglary and Theft Coverage: Coverage afforded on all home policies that covers items in the event they are stolen. If the stolen items are later recovered, the insurance company may recover payments made under this coverage from the insured or may recover the salvage value of such items if they are found damaged.

Catastrophe: An occurrence such as a natural disaster or widespread fire in which such a high number of claims are related to one disaster that it can be statistically ruled as catastrophic. Catastrophe, or cat, claims, are forgiven by some insurance companies — if this is the case, these claims do not create any increase in rates.

Coverage: A term that is sometimes used instead of insurance. Coverage applies to all risks eligible for payment under an insurance policy. Coverage can also be used to describe one part of a policy that provides payment for a unique type of loss, such as burglary and theft, flood, or crime.

Covered Loss: An occurrence that causes damage or loss to your home or personal property which is eligible for claim payment under an insurance policy. For an occurrence to be considered a covered loss, the policy must have been in force at the time the loss occurred, and no exclusions may apply to the loss.

Credit Scores: Numerical representations of a policyholder's creditworthiness that are provided by the three major credit reporting bureaus — Experian, Equifax, and TransUnion. Credit scores are sometimes obtained and used by insurers for determining eligibility for coverage and for determining appropriate premiums payable for insurance coverage.

Crime Insurance: A term for coverage afforded for losses occurring as a result of theft, burglary or other illegal act that was not committed by the insured or at the direction of the insured.

Declarations Page: Sometimes referred to as a "dec page," this is a document that shows policyholder information, the address of the insured property, insurance premiums due for the policy term, effective and expiration dates of the policy term, and policy coverages and limits. In most states, a declarations page is considered part of the policy and can be used in hearings and trials to prove coverage for a loss.

Deductible: The out-of-pocket amount the insured is responsible for when a claim is filed. This amount must be paid before coverage can be afforded for a loss. For example, if the deductible is $500 and $2,000 worth of damage has been incurred, the insured pays the first $500 of the loss, and the insurance company pays the remaining $1,500.

Deductibles help to keep premium costs down by requiring the policyholder to retain a portion of the risk of loss and by reducing the amount an insurance company pays for adjusting and administrating expenses for small losses.

Earthquake Insurance: Coverage for damage or loss caused by an earthquake. This hazard is not covered on a basic homeowner's insurance policy but can be added for an additional premium amount. This coverage is a good idea if you live in an earthquake-prone area but is not essential in many parts of the United States.

Electronic Commerce or E-Commerce Policies: Legally valid insurance policies that can be purchased online. Insurance companies that sell policies online may provide tools to help you determine the coverages you need and the type of policy you need to protect your financial well-being. When you purchase a policy online, you can download and print your declarations page immediately after paying your policy premium.

Electronic Signature: A means by which a policy applicant or policyholder demonstrates agreement with the terms and conditions of an insurance policy without physically signing paper documents. Federal and state laws are not yet clear regarding what actions are needed to make an electronic signature carry the same legal weight as a paper signature.

Endorsements or Riders: Documents that can be attached to an insurance policy to add coverages not otherwise included on the policy. They are often used to add specialty coverages to a policy or increase the number or nature of the perils covered.

Escrow Accounts: Temporary holding accounts that allow a mortgage company to pay home insurance premiums to an insurance company and add the cost of insurance into the monthly mortgage payment. This benefits homeowners by allowing them to make a single payment to cover their mortgage loans and insurance policy premiums. It also benefits insurance companies because they can be assured premiums will be paid as long as the homeowner is making timely mortgage payments.

Exclusion: A statement contained within an insurance policy, endorsement, or rider that identifies a certain risk not covered by the policy. Exclusions are specifically listed in your insurance policy and can be invalidated only if they violate state or federal law.

Exposure: An increased possibility that a loss will occur. Insurance companies evaluate exposures to determine both the insurability of a property and the premiums that will be charged for accepting the risk.

Extended Coverage: An addition or endorsement to the policy that provides coverage the policy would not normally provide.

Extended Replacement Cost Coverage: A policy coverage or rider that pays a set additional amount over the policy limit to rebuild or replace a damaged home.

Fair Access to Insurance Requirements Plans/FAIR Plans: Plans that provide property insurance to people for properties that do not qualify for coverage with standard insurance companies. These plans are administered by state governments, although certain facets of these plans are mandated by federal law.

Fire Insurance: A policy that provides coverage for an insured property in the event it is damaged due to fire or lightning.

Floater: Coverage that can be added to a home policy to cover movable property wherever the loss occurs. Floaters are sometimes added for valuable jewelry, furs, and musical instruments.

Flood Insurance: Coverage that is provided by the federal government to insure a home damaged by flood. Flood insurance is excluded on all home policies, but the government plan can be purchased through any licensed agent, agency, or insurance company that writes home insurance.

Forced Place Insurance: Coverage that can be purchased by a mortgage company or bank, on the homeowner's behalf, to insure an uninsured property. This protects the mortgage company's or bank's investment in the event of a loss but does not provide any coverage or liability protection for the homeowner. This type of policy is often costly for the homeowner and can be added to the cost of the mortgage loan without the homeowner's consent.

Fraud: An act committed when the policyholder intentionally lies or withholds the truth from an insurance company in an attempt to receive payment for a claim.

Grace Period: An additional time, given by an insurance company after the policy premium due date, during which the insured may make payments to avoid cancellation of the policy for nonpayment.

Guaranteed Replacement Cost Coverage: Guarantees the entire replacement cost to rebuild a home will be paid under an insurance policy, even if the cost exceeds the policy limit.

Hurricane Deductible: The set amount of money the insured must pay out of pocket before the insurance policy pays the remaining amount of a loss caused by a hurricane.

Identity Theft Coverage: An additional coverage that can be purchased to pay expenses incurred in the event the policyholder's identity is stolen. Identity theft coverage can be purchased as a standalone policy or as part of another insurance policy. Some companies offer this coverage as an endorsement on a home policy.

Inflation Guard Clause: A part of an insurance policy or rider that automatically adjusts the coverage on a home to keep up with inflation and increased building costs. This helps prevent situations in which home insurance policy limits are made insufficient to pay for a loss because of inflation.

Inland Marine Policies: Policies that can be purchased to provide additional coverage for expensive jewelry, musical instruments, and furs. Initially, this coverage was designed to cover valuable personal property while it was being transported, but today, it is used to provide coverage for personal property.

Insurable Interest: A legal interest that is created when a party has a financial stake in the property. A mortgage holder has insurable interest in a property because it owns the loan for the property and would be compromised by the homeowner's inability to pay the mortgage loan.

Insurance Score: A numerical value calculated by an insurance company using credit information that aids in the rating of the insurance policy. An insurance score differs from a credit score because the values are determined by the insurer rather than by a credit rating bureau.

Insurance-To-Value: A type of coverage written based on the approximate value of the insured property, when a full appraisal has not been conducted to determine the actual value of the property.

Internet Insurer: An insurance company or group of companies that sells insurance policies solely online. Internet insurers may offer all of the same coverages available on a policy purchased through an agent. The primary difference between an Internet insurer and a traditional insurer is you can receive quotes and purchase policies online, without the need for visiting an insurance agency.

Lapse: A break in coverage that occurs when premium is not paid by the end of the grace period, causing the policy to cancel for nonpayment. Insurance companies may provide a reinstatement period during which you may restore coverage under your policy without having to start a new policy and having your property subject to underwriting and appraisals. Any loss that occurs during a coverage lapse will not be eligible for payment under your policy.

Liability Insurance: Insurance that covers the insured for property damage or injury caused to others.

Limits: The maximum amounts an insurer will pay out for a covered loss, subject to deductibles and payments made under another insurance policy.

Line of Insurance: A specific kind of insurance designed to cover a particular group of hazards or insure particular types of property or people. For example, home insurance is considered a personal line of property and casualty insurance.

Loss: An accident, damage, theft, vandalism, or disaster that causes a decrease in the value of property, loss of personal property, or a liability for which the homeowner is legally responsible.

Loss of Use: Financial loss that occurs when a home is unlivable, or personal property is unusable, due to a covered loss. Payment for loss of use is made for alternate housing or temporary replacement of personal property while repairs are being made. For loss of use coverage to apply, an expense must be one that the policyholder would not have incurred if the damage to the home or personal property would not have occurred.

Medical Payments: Coverage that can be paid, up to the policy limit, if someone is injured on the insured property, even if it is not a result of the insured's actions.

Mine Subsidence Coverage: Insurance that can be added to home policies in some states to cover the home if it is damaged due to land under the home sinking into a mine shaft.

Mortgage Insurance: A policy that can be purchased to pay off the remainder of a mortgage in the event of the policyholder's death. Mortgage insurance can also be used to pay a policyholder's mortgage payments during a period of disability, when the policyholder is unable to work because of injury or specified illness.

Named Peril: A peril specifically listed on the insurance policy. Fire, wind, and hail are all examples of named perils.

National Flood Insurance Program: The program provided by the federal government that allows homeowners to purchase flood insurance for a home located in a designated flood zone.

Notice of Loss: A written notification, required by the insurance company, notifying the company of a loss.

Ordinance of Law: A coverage that can be added to a homeowner's policy to replace or repair the home to bring structural elements, mechanicals, plumbing, or electrical wiring and connections into compliance with current legal standards. This is necessary for older homes that were built before modern building codes were in existence.

Personal Article Floaters: Additional coverages that can be purchased or added to a policy to insure valuable items, such as jewelry and furs.

Personal Lines Insurance: A subset of property and casualty insurance that includes automobile and home insurance. Coverages available under personal lines insurance are purchased by individuals to cover their personal property.

Policy: The written and agreed on contract, drafted by the insurance company and executed by both the insured and insurer, providing coverage on the property.

Premises: The specific property being insured, including buildings, land, fences, swimming pools, and other features of the property.

Premium: The money due from the insured in exchange for the coverage extended by the insurer. Premiums are determined by assessing the characteristics of the property as well as the activities of the person owning and insuring the property.

Proof of Loss: Written documentation of proof that a loss occurred.

Property and Casualty Insurance: The classification of insurance that provides auto, home, and commercial lines of coverage. Regulation of property and casualty insurance is much different than regulation for life, health, and other lines of insurance.

Rate: The cost of a unit of insurance used to determine the premiums that individual policyholders will pay. Unless an insurer is operating in a state where rates are determined by the Department of Insurance, rates are normally calculated by use of statistical data and loss history.

Rate Regulation: The monitoring of an insurance company's rates by the state's insurance department. Some states require an opportunity to review an insurer's rates before they are used; others require rates to be filed on or before the date that they are used. A few states still decide the rates that insurers must charge and force every insurer writing business in those states to use the same rate structure.

In recent years, aggressive rate regulation has been discouraged by insurance advisory groups. Instead, a market-based system is being promoted, in which insurers are free to determine their own rates, so long as they do not place rates so low as to jeopardize their ability to pay claims.

Reinstatement: Allowed within a certain time period after policy cancellation to put the policy back in force by paying a fee.

Renter's or Tenant's Insurance: Coverage that can be purchased by those who rent their home to cover their personal belongings against a loss.

Replacement Cost: The actual amount of money it would take to rebuild a home or replace personal property after a covered loss occurs. Coverage purchased on a replacement cost basis may be more expensive than coverage purchased on an actual cash value basis, because the insurance company could pay out substantially more than the property is worth if significant depreciation of the property has occurred.

Risk: The probability of a loss occurring. Each person bears a certain amount of risk by owning a home or inviting guests into the home. Risk can be mitigated by taking steps to make sure the property is in good condition; sidewalks, decks, and other features of the home are in good repair; and the home is constructed of fire-resistant materials.

Scheduled Items: Specific items of value listed on the policy. The value of each item will be listed, whether it is calculated by the insurance company or stated by the insured.

Sewer Backup Coverage: Coverage that can be added to a home policy to insure against loss occurring due to the backup of sewers and drains.

Territorial Rating: Rating based on the particular geographic area where the home is located. Certain areas are considered to have higher risks of theft, damage, and disaster than others. Territorial rating may be determined by using statistical data available from insurance advisory organizations or by using the insurer's own loss experience in different geographic areas.

Umbrella Policy: A policy or rider that can be purchased to extend higher limits of liability coverage over an auto and homeowner's policy in case a large loss occurs. Umbrella policy limits normally start at $1 million.

Uninsurable Risk: A risk that makes acceptance of the policy difficult because the insurance company views the risk as being too great. Owners of properties that are considered uninsurable risks may need to seek coverage under the FAIR Plan of the state where the property is located.

Vandalism: The act of intentional damage to, or destruction of, another person's property.

Writing a Policy: The insurer's

act of accepting an application for an insurance policy and entering into a contractual agreement with the insured to provide coverage for covered losses.

AUTOMOBILE INSURANCE TERMINOLOGY

Acquisition Expense Load: A charge assessed by an insurance company during the first term of a policy to recoup acquisition expenses, such as marketing, underwriting, and agent commissions. Unlike a policy fee, an acquisition expense load is expressed as a percentage of the first-term policy premiums, so the higher your premium, the higher the acquisition expense load will be.

At-Fault Accident: If you are involved in an accident and are issued a citation showing you as being responsible for the accident, it is considered an at-fault accident. In many states, any claims for an accident will be filed with the insurance company of the person who is at fault for the accident.

Auto ID Card: An auto identification card will be provided on the date the policy begins and at each policy renewal. This ID card should remain in the vehicle and will serve as proof of insurance if you are in an accident or pulled over for a traffic violation.

Auto Loss History Report (ALH Report): This report is run by your insurance company to obtain your claims history. This report will also show record of your previous insurance companies.

Billing Fee: Some insurance companies will add an extra billing fee to each installment paid if you choose to be on a monthly or quarterly billing plan instead of paying for the entire term when starting the policy or renewing. Some companies will waive this billing fee if you set your payments up to be automatically withdrawn monthly.

Cancellation: An action taken by an insurer to terminate coverage under an insurance policy before the expiration date of the policy term. In most states, an insurer may cancel your policy within the stated underwriting period for any reason other than age, race, gender, marital status, religion, or personal creed. After the underwriting period, an insurance company can cancel your policy only for reasons stated by the laws of that state. An insurance company must provide written notice before canceling your policy to give you an opportunity to find other coverage.

Claimant: If a policyholder damages a person's property or causes injury to occur as the result of an accident, this person can file a claim on his or her insurance policy. The named insured and additional insureds may also be claimants for first-party coverages.

Comprehensive Loss Underwriting Exchange (CLUE) Reports: Reports provided by ChoicePoint that are used by insurance companies to assess the risk of a prospective applicant or policyholder. These reports contain information such as policyholder name, policy number, and dates and amounts of claims made under previous policies. CLUE reports do not contain traffic citations or other information not directly related to a property claim made under a policy.

Declarations Page: A declarations page lists the vehicles insured on a policy, the coverage provided for each vehicle, and the premiums paid for each coverage. A declarations page is provided at each term renewal.

Earned Premium: The portion of your auto insurance premiums that your insurance company has earned at a specific time during the policy period. For example, if you pay for a policy period of six months and you are at the end of your second month of the policy term, your insurance company has earned one-third of your policy premium. This is important because if you or your insurer cancels your policy, any refund to you will be based on what is left after earned premium and fees have been deducted from your premium payment.

First Party Benefits: Coverages that are designed to protect you or other people insured under your policy, rather than to protect you against liability to others. These can include medical expenses, accidental death benefits, and rehabilitation services.

Grace Period: Some insurance companies will offer a grace period of several days for policyholders to pay their bill after the due date. During this time, the policy will remain active and a reinstatement fee will not be collected.

Installment Fee: An assessment that is charged by an insurer for the privilege of making your premium payments in installments, instead of paying for the entire policy term at once. This fee may be charged with each installment payment you make — the greater the number of installment payments you choose to make over a policy term, the more you will spend on installment fees.

Insurance Score: An insurance score is determined for each person on a policy. This score determines the rates for an individual by factoring in driving record and claims. Age, sex, marital status, and maintaining an insurance policy with no lapse in coverage can also factor in when determining rates.

Interpolicy Stacking: The ability to combine limits from two or more policies. For example, if two policies apply to the same policyholder, interpolicy stacking would allow the policyholder to add the policy limits for both policies to determine the total coverage limit for an accident. Some states limit interpolicy stacking to policies issued by the same insurance company or different affiliates of the same insurance company.

Intrapolicy Stacking: The ability to combine limits from different vehicles on the same policy to determine the total policy limit for an accident. For example, if a policyholder held an auto insurance policy with three vehicles, intrapolicy stacking would allow the policyholder to add the policy limits applicable to all three vehicles to determine the total coverage limit for one accident. Intrapolicy stacking may only apply to uninsured motorist bodily injury and underinsured motorist bodily injury coverages and is available in only a handful of states.

Lapse in Coverage: A lapse in insurance coverage can occur when a policy cancels for nonpayment of premium and is later reinstated. There is no coverage for any accidents or losses that occurred on the dates during which the policy was canceled.

Late Fee: Many insurance companies will charge a late fee for any premium payments that are received after the due date. States may place a limit on the amount insurance companies may charge for this fee, either as a total dollar amount per late payment or as a percentage of the premium due but paid late.

Liability: Your legal responsibility for damages caused to another person because of your actions as a driver. These damages are classified as bodily injury liability (physical injury to occupants of another vehicle, pedestrians, or bystanders) or property damage liability (damage caused to an automobile or the personal property of others). By providing liability coverage, an insurance company assumes your financial responsibility for damages you cause to others. An insurer's assumption of your liability may not be subject to the same number of exclusions as its assumption of your risk of damage to your own property or physical well-being.

Motor Vehicle Report (MVR): A report obtained by an insurance company or affiliate from a state's motor vehicle department that contains information about citations issued to a driver during the three years before the date of the report. Insurers use MVRs to verify driver violations and to adjust premium rates for an insurance policy during an underwriting period or renewal period.

Nonrenewal: An action taken by an insurer to decline to continue coverage after the expiration of a policy period. While an insurance company is limited in the reasons it can cancel your policy during a policy period, most states allow an insurance company to not renew a policy for any reason other than age, race, gender, marital status, religion, or personal creed.

Nonstandard Policy: Also called a high-risk policy, this automobile insurance policy is characterized by liberal acceptance guidelines, moderate to high policy premiums, and highly restrictive coverage. This type of policy is an option for drivers who cannot obtain coverage elsewhere, have a history of frequent citations or losses, have a poor credit history, or have never had automobile insurance coverage.

Not-At-Fault Accident: If someone else causes an accident with a policyholder, the accident will be classified as not at fault.

Physical Damage: Damage that occurs to an automobile or personal property as a result of an accident, theft, or vandalism.

Policy Period: The length of a given term of your policy. Many automobile insurance policies have renewable policy terms of six months; others provide policy periods of 12 months. Unless you are within the underwriting period of your first policy term with an insurance company or an affiliate of an insurance company, an insurer cannot raise your premiums during a policy period unless you add a driver or a vehicle to your policy.

Policy Fee: A charge made by an insurance company during the first policy period of your automobile insurance policy to recoup expenses associated with marketing, underwriting, and agent commissions. A policy fee differs from an acquisition expense load in that it is a set amount for each policy, rather than being a percentage of a policyholder's first policy term premiums. An insurance company cannot charge you both an acquisition expense load and a policy fee for the same policy.

Premium Finance Company: A company that finances a policyholder's premiums so the policyholder can make installment payments, rather than paying the entire policy period premium at once. Premium finance companies charge interest for amounts not yet paid for the policy period — the interest may be on par with credit card interest rates. These companies are becoming less common because insurers are becoming increasingly willing to allow premiums to be paid in installments — essentially, to finance the premiums themselves.

Rebating: Rebating is an illegal practice in insurance that occurs when an insurance agent reduces his or her commission to give you a lower rate or provides gifts to entice you to buy a policy.

Redlining: Redlining is an illegal practice that occurs when an agent or company refuses coverage to individuals because they live in a specific geographic area.

Reinstatement Fee: If a policy is canceled due to nonpayment of premium, a reinstatement fee may be collected. States may limit the amount insurance companies can charge to reinstate a lapsed policy. Once this fee is paid, the policy will be made active again, but there will be a lapse in coverage between the cancel date and the date the reinstatement fee was paid.

Renewal Period: A specified number of days at the end of a policy period when an insurance company reevaluates an automobile insurance policy to determine premium rates and eligibility for the next policy period. During the renewal period, insurance companies may obtain MVRs, CLUE reports, credit reports, or other sources of driver information to assist them in determining renewal premiums and continued driver eligibility.

Rescission: An action taken by an insurance company that cancels an automobile insurance policy back to the inception date. When an insurer rescinds a policy, it is as if the policy had never existed. States may not allow insurance companies to rescind a policy except in cases of material misrepresentation or fraud or cases in which a policyholder's initial premium payment is dishonored by the bank or other financial institution on which it is drawn.

Standard Policy: Also called a preferred risk policy, this type of automobile insurance policy is characterized by moderate to stringent acceptability guidelines, low premiums, and generous coverage. Insurance companies keep the premiums low for these policies by accepting only applicants with clean or nearly clean driving records, a history of infrequent or no losses, and a good credit score.

Subrogation: If a policyholder is not at fault for an accident but does not know who is responsible for the damage to his or her vehicle or simply has inadequate contact or insurance information, he or she can choose to file a claim for repairs on his or her own policy. The insurance company will pay the claim but will attempt to find

the insurance company of the at-fault party to get its money back. The policyholder will be subject to the deductible but has a chance to get reimbursed for the deductible amount after the claim is settled with the insurance company of the at-fault driver.

Total Loss: A total loss occurs when the damage to a vehicle would cost more to repair than the actual cash value of the vehicle at the time of the accident or loss. The policyholder is paid the actual cash value of the vehicle, but the vehicle is not repaired.

Underwriting Period: A specified number of days at the beginning of your initial policy period with an insurance company during which an insurer may adjust your premiums due to information derived from a covered driver's MVR, CLUE report, credit report, or other information source. An insurance company may also cancel or rescind your policy during the underwriting period if the insurer obtains information about a driver or vehicle that would have caused the insurer to decline the policy had the information been divulged during the application process. State laws mandate the length of the underwriting period — most states limit the period to 60 or 90 days.

Underwriting reports: Reports run by your insurance company to help determine your insurance score. These reports may include your MVR, CLUE report, ALH, and consumer credit report.

Unearned premium: The portion of your policy premium payment that your insurance company has yet to earn at a specific time during your policy period. For example, if you pay for a six-month policy and you are at the end of the second month of the policy term, two-thirds of your premium payment is unearned premium. This is important because, if you or your insurance company cancels your policy during the policy term, your refund will be comprised of the unearned premium, less any cancellation fees.

Vehicle Identification Number (VIN): Each motor vehicle manufactured after 1970 has a unique VIN that corresponds with the vehicle's year, make, model, and security features. It is important to have this number available when adding a vehicle to your policy or obtaining quotes so that you will receive an accurate rate. Insurance companies use software that reads the VIN of a vehicle to determine its year, make, model, and features for rating and acceptability purposes.

Vehicle inspection: Many insurance companies will ask you to bring your vehicle in to be inspected at the time the policy starts. A vehicle inspection will show any damage that was on the vehicle before coverage in the event that a policyholder would try to make a claim on damage done to the vehicle before the policy started.

HEALTH INSURANCE TERMINOLOGY

Acute Care: Skilled healthcare provided by nurses and doctors that is medically necessary to restore you to health, such as medical care required after major surgery.

Benefits Period: The time during which you are eligible for benefits under your health insurance policy. For example, if you are hospitalized for an illness, the benefits period may begin on the day you are admitted to the hospital and end 60 days after you are released.

Coinsurance: The amount of your healthcare costs that you are required to pay before coverage under your health insurance policy begins. Coinsurance is expressed as a percentage of the costs for a particular healthcare service (for example, 20 percent of hospital services or urgent care costs).

Co-payment: The amount of your healthcare costs that you are required to pay before coverage under your health insurance policy begins. Copayments are expressed as specific dollar amounts for some types of coverage (for example, $20 for a doctor's office visit or $10 for a prescription).

Consolidated Omnibus Budget Reconciliation Act (COBRA): A federal act passed by the United States in 1986 that allows employees to continue health insurance coverage in most circumstances on leaving a job. If you are terminated for gross misconduct, you will not be eligible to continue your coverage under COBRA. The length of time you will be able to continue your health coverage through the same insurance policy varies depending on the reason for separation from your employer.

Deductible: A specific dollar amount that you are required to pay before health insurance benefits begin covering your healthcare costs. Many health insurance policies feature both a deductible and a co-payment for services other than prescriptions and doctor's office visits.

Elimination Period: A time, maybe expressed in days, during which your stay at a long-term treatment facility will not be covered. The elimination period is sometimes referred to as a time deductible, because you are expected to pay for the first part of your long-term care treatment.

Enrollment Period: Health insurance available through employers can be obtained or modified only during a specific time period set each year by your plan's administrator. Many companies choose the month of December as the enrollment period, so employees can begin their health coverage at the beginning of the next year. New employees and people who experience qualifying events may be able to begin or modify their health insurance coverage at other times during the year.

Excess Major Medical Policy: A health insurance policy with a high policy limit — $2 million or more — designed to cover medical expenses after other health insurance coverage has been exhausted. Excess major medical policies may have high deductibles — some policies carry deductibles of $5,000 or more.

Formulary: A medication that appears on a health insurer's list of approved medications under a particular plan. Your health insurer will not pay for prescriptions or over-the-counter medications that do not appear on the formulary list.

Freedom of Choice Plan: A health insurance plan in which you have the ability to choose the doctor or specialist right for your family's needs. If you or a member of your family becomes ill, this type of plan will allow you to seek out a specialist that can best diagnose and treat the condition. The chances of success in curing the illness are significantly better with a freedom of choice plan than with a managed care plan, because you have the ability to select the top specialist to meet your healthcare needs. Premiums under this type of plan are higher than those paid for managed care plans.

Health Maintenance Organization (HMO): A physician organization set up to manage healthcare costs, designed to provide medical services to patients as affordably as possible. HMOs focus extensively on preventative care and often use incentives such as the waiver of deductible or co-payment requirements to encourage patients to seek preventative care to avoid illness and injury. Many HMOs own the clinics in which their doctors operate and provide limited or no nonemergency coverage for treatment obtained outside the clinic without a referral.

Hospice Care: Medical and nursing services provided to terminally ill patients. These services may be provided in the patient's home, in a nursing care facility, or in a hospice center. Hospice care is designed to keep the patient comfortable during his or her last days and to allow family members, social workers, and religious leaders to visit regularly.

Major Medical Coverage: A health insurance policy that has high policy limits designed to cover most serious illnesses and injuries that require extensive medical care. The high limits offered under major medical policies also allow for ongoing treatment of long-term health issues, such as chronic diseases and syndromes.

Managed Care Plan: A health insurance plan under which your insurance company designates the doctors, specialists, and other providers you may use to treat a particular condition. Under a managed care plan, you may request referrals from your primary care physician; however, your insurance company is not obligated to approve the referral request. Managed care plans may also limit you to doctors and specialists in your home territory, except for emergency care, so coverage while you are on vacation or otherwise away from home may be significantly limited.

Medicaid: In the United States, Medicaid is a health insurance program regulated on the federal and state levels that is available to individuals with incomes below certain levels. This program also pays for nursing home care for indigent elderly people and mentally disabled individuals.

Medicare: A federally mandated health insurance program designed to provide healthcare benefits to people who are over 65 years of age, certain people with total disabilities, and people with permanent kidney failure.

Out-of-Pocket Maximum: This feature of health insurance policies caps the maximum amount per year you will pay for deductibles and copayments. Many health insurance policies have a per-person out-of-pocket maximum and a separate per-family maximum.

Preferred Provider Organization (PPO): A group of doctors and hospitals that agree to operate under cost and managed care controls set by a health insurance company. PPOs allow health insurance companies to manage claims costs and keep premiums as low as possible, because the doctors and hospitals have agreed to provide medical services at reduced costs in exchange for their preferred status. Choosing a PPO plan can be a good choice for minimizing health insurance premiums if you do not have a preference regarding which doctors and hospitals you use to meet your healthcare needs.

Preventative Care: Medical and healthcare that is designed to prevent illnesses, rather than treat existing illnesses. Preventative care includes measures such as routine checkups, diagnostic tests, immunizations, and wellness training.

Primary Care Physician: A doctor who provides basic services to patients and refers patients to specialists when necessary. Many PPOs and HMOs require insured people to select and establish relationships with their primary care physicians. HMOs assign primary care physicians to patients to act as gatekeepers — that is, to keep medical services in house as long as possible — to help reduce medical costs.

Qualifying Event: An event that allows an employee to begin, modify, or terminate his or her health insurance coverage outside the enrollment period designated by the employer's plan administrator. These events include marriage, divorce, death, and the birth of a child.

Respite Care: When a patient is receiving hospice care, respite care may be provided to family members to give them a break from the emotional and physical strain of caring for a terminally ill patient. Respite care involves temporarily admitting the patient to a hospice care or nursing facility or sending nursing professionals to the patient's home for a short time.

LIFE INSURANCE TERMINOLOGY

Beneficiary: The person or entity who will receive the proceeds of your life insurance policy in the event of your death. The beneficiary of a life insurance policy is the policyholder's spouse or children, although a company may be designated as a beneficiary if the policy is pledged as collateral or to improve the policyholder's credit rating.

Child Life Insurance: A life insurance policy designed to provide parents with a death benefit if a child passes away before reaching adulthood. Some child life insurance policies can be converted into traditional life insurance policies once a child reaches the age of majority.

Decreasing Term: A term life insurance policy in which the premium stays the same throughout the life of the policy, but the benefit amount steadily decreases. These policies can be used to cover mortgage loans, installment loans, or other types of financial obligations that decrease in amount over time.

Dividends: Payments issued to policyholders by a mutual insurance company if the company makes a profit. The amount a policyholder receives as a dividend is based on the face value of the insurance policy owned by the policyholder.

Group Life Insurance: A life insurance policy that covers a group of people, rather than a single individual or a family. Group life insurance policies are provided by an employer at little or no cost to employees. These policies will sometimes provide a death benefit for the employee's spouse as well as the employee. This coverage is not portable — once the employee leaves the company, all coverage under the group policy is terminated.

Level Term: A term insurance policy in which the benefit amount stays the same throughout the life of the policy. These policies may be rated on an annual renewable basis, which raises the premium each year the policy is in force, or on a level basis, which keeps premium payments the same throughout the life of the policy.

Mutual Insurance Company: An insurance company that is owned by its policyholders, rather than a group of shareholders. If a mutual company makes a profit during a given year, it will issue dividends to its policyholders. These dividends may be used to offset or reduce premiums or to purchase additional coverage.

Stock Company: An insurance company that is owned by its shareholders, rather than its policyholders. Unlike a mutual company, a stock company does not pay dividends to policyholders but instead pays a portion of its profits to shareholders. Unless you happen to own stock in the insurance company, you will not receive any money back if the company profits.

Term Insurance: A life insurance policy that is designed to meet a short-term financial need. Term insurance policies are often used to cover a mortgage, installment loan, or other financial obligation with an established end date. These policies pay out only if the insured person dies within the policy term. Term insurance policies may be converted to whole life policies at any time the term policy is in force.

Universal Life: A type of life insurance policy that provides a death benefit similar to a whole life policy but also provides a means for you to invest a portion of your premium payments in a cash value account. Universal life policies guarantee a certain interest rate on the cash value of your account and may pay additional interest on your cash value if the company's operations are profitable.

Variable Universal Life: A variant of the traditional universal life policy which provides the same death benefit and opportunity for investment. Unlike a traditional universal life policy, the company does not guarantee an interest percentage. Instead, you have the ability to place the cash value of your policy in separate accounts that act as mutual funds. This gives you the opportunity for greater gain than is available through a traditional universal life policy but also the chance of losing money in your cash value account.

Whole Life: A life insurance policy that is designed to provide benefits until the policyholder reaches age 100. This policy must accumulate a cash value after the third year and pays the face value or the cash value of the policy, whichever is more, if the policyholder lives to age 100. If the policyholder dies before age 100, the policy pays the face value.

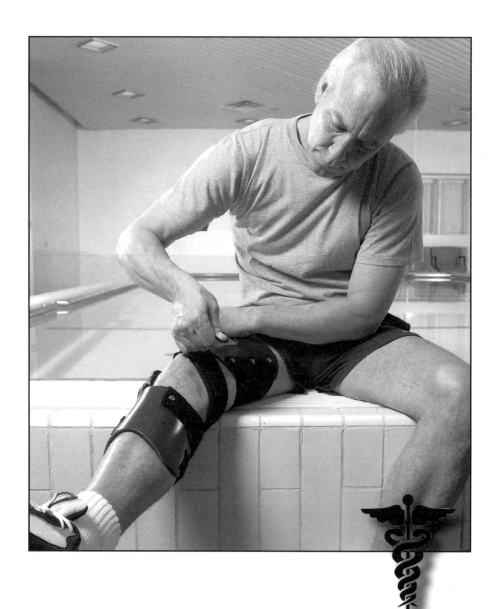

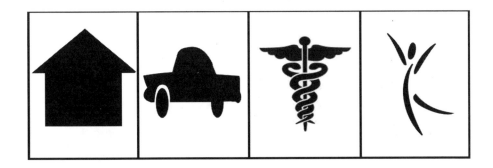

APPENDIX C: OTHER RESOURCES

Here you will find several resources that you can use to gain additional information about specific insurance companies and insurance topics.

A.M. BEST

www.ambest.com

A.M. Best is a company that collects information about insurance companies and provides a financial strength rating for each. Companies with a financial strength rating of A or A+ are considered the most financially sound companies and have a strong capacity to handle claims submitted by policyholders and third parties.

FINDLAW

www.findlaw.com

FindLaw is a free service you can use to research insurance laws in each state. State statutes are set up in easy-to-navigate tables of contents, so you can quickly find laws related to your insurance concerns.

INSURANCE INFORMATION INSTITUTE

www.iii.org

This Web site contains news releases about topics affecting insurance consumers and insurers. It also contains a wealth of information geared toward educating consumers about various insurance topics.

INSURE.COM

www.insure.com

You can use the resources available on this Web site to find out which insurance companies write the most business in your state. **Insure.com** also contains a number of informative articles to help you gain knowledge about a number of consumer-related insurance topics.

NATIONAL ASSOCIATION OF INSURANCE COMMISSIONERS

www.naic.org

You can use the Consumer Information Source on this Web site to find out which insurance companies write business in your state and review the financial statements published by insurance companies each year. You can also find information on insurance topics and on legislation that may affect your ability to purchase and maintain insurance.

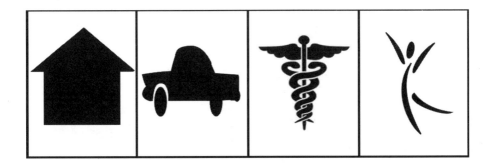

APPENDIX D: CASE STUDIES

On the following pages, you will find a number of Case Studies completed by insurance professionals and consumers. These Case Studies will show you how consumers like you have navigated the sometimes difficult process of obtaining affordable insurance and how insurance professionals feel about the current state of the insurance industry.

As you will see, different people have different ideas about how to best obtain insurance that meets your budget and your family's needs. Use the information and suggestions contained in these Case Studies to gather additional ideas for preparing to look for quotes, obtaining necessary coverages, and dealing with insurance agents. You may find a tip or suggestion that helps you save money the next time you shop for an insurance policy to protect you and your family.

CASE STUDY: TIFFANY R.

Columbus, Ohio

One of the most important techniques I have used to lower the costs of my insurance policies is to examine the individual coverages in "packages" offered by insurance agents. For example, I rejected rental coverage on my automobile insurance policy because I have a second vehicle I can use if my primary vehicle breaks down or is damaged.

Also, I noticed my homeowner's insurance package included coverage for basement flooding and sump pump backup. Since I do not have a basement or a sump pump, I asked my agent to remove that coverage. Analyzing your policies to identify coverages you do not need can save you quite a bit of money on your insurance premiums.

There are a few steps you can take before you begin gathering quotes to make sure you are getting the best rates available. For example, before you start getting automobile insurance quotes, get a copy of your motor vehicle report and dispute any inaccuracies. There is no sense in paying for a ticket you never received. Also, make sure you gather copies of any current policies, so you can compare quotes you receive with the coverages you already have and the premiums you are already paying.

Even if you already have insurance, I would recommend continuing to shop around. This does not have to be a continual process — you can start shopping about three months before your current policy term expires. You may end up staying with your current company, but it is a good idea to see if other companies have more competitive rates.

One of the best things you can do to lower your insurance rates is to use common sense in all of your decisions. You can avoid accidents by not talking on your cell phone, applying makeup, or changing the station on your car stereo while driving. Avoiding these activities will help improve your driving record and may even save your life.

CASE STUDY: ANNA MARIE F.

Westerville, Ohio

Many people choose to shop around quite a bit for insurance coverages, but the downside of this is that if you frequently change companies or insurance programs, you may miss out on discounts you may receive by staying with a particular company.

CASE STUDY: ANNA MARIE F.

I recommend that if you find an agent who is able to provide you with the coverage you want at a cost you can live with, you stay with that agent and company as long as possible, especially if your company offers discounts for each policy renewal.

In fact, more insurance companies should offer discounts to people who stay with them and do not file frequent claims. The availability of these discounts would be an incentive for people to think twice before submitting a claim or hopping insurance companies. This would help build a more stable insurance market that is both profitable for insurance companies and affordable for consumers.

Another thing that insurance companies could do to lower the costs of insurance for consumers would be to reduce the amount of paperwork printed and mailed to customers and concentrate instead on making policy-related materials available via the Internet. This would cut down on insurance company administrative costs, and companies could pass these savings along to consumers.

CASE STUDY: BETTY P.

New Castle, Indiana

One of the best ways I have found for lowering my insurance premiums is to place as many types of insurance as possible with the same company and agent. Not only can you obtain multiline discounts by having more than one policy with the same company, but you can obtain little-known information from your agent by placing several policies with his or her agency. After all, if an agent knows he or she will lose several policies if you decide to take your insurance business elsewhere, the agent will work harder to keep you happy.

Once you find an agent you can trust, ask him or her for opinions on what coverages would best meet your needs. Do not let your agent assume you are an average customer with the same needs as everyone else. Each person has a unique financial situation that requires a unique combination of insurance coverages.

Overall, the most important thing you can do to lower your insurance rates is to find an agent who will work hard to meet your needs, and stick with that agent. There is always a new company showing up, advertising lower rates, but it often will not offer you the protection you need or the rates it advertises.

In my opinion, one of the best things insurance companies could do to lower the costs of insurance coverage for consumers is to significantly limit the salaries and perks available to insurance company CEOs.

CASE STUDY: KEN R.

New Holland, Ohio

I have been successful in obtaining lower insurance premiums by carefully listening to other consumers who recommend particular companies or agents. If you consistently hear good things about a company or agent, you can bet you will receive good service and the agent will take care of you by finding ways for you to save money on your insurance policies.

In recent years, insurance companies seem to have become more willing to provide financial incentives to encourage people to become better risks. For example, automobile insurance companies have begun offering discounts to seniors who take driver improvement courses — this helps older drivers brush up on their skills so they can avoid accidents. In turn, this helps older drivers lower their insurance rates.

Insurance companies have also taken other steps to help people become better risks. For example, my health insurance company recently launched a campaign to promote a 24-hour hotline that policyholders can call with questions about health-related concerns. The hotline is staffed by nurses and specialists, so policyholders can be assured they are receiving quality information.

One of the best things I think consumers can do to lower insurance rates is to make more rational, less extravagant choices. Instead of buying the most expensive, most impressive vehicle you can afford, concentrate on selecting a vehicle that is inexpensive to insure. Instead of purchasing a huge house with rooms you will not use, purchase a more modest house — it will be substantially cheaper to insure.

CASE STUDY: ANN B.

McArthur, Ohio

My husband and I have used the same agent and company to provide our insurance needs for many years. Over the years, our agent has made numerous suggestions that have helped us save money on our insurance premiums.

For example, several years ago, our agent noticed we were not using approximately one half of our house. Because our house is long, he noted any fire that occurred in the house would not likely burn down the entire structure. He was able to reduce our coverage on the part of our home we do not use, which helped save a substantial amount on our home insurance premiums.

CASE STUDY: ANN B.

One thing you can do to help save money before you start calling agents for quotes is to make your own assessment of what types of coverage you need and in what amounts. Your agent will do his or her best to assess your needs, but you must be willing to make the final determination so you do not end up with coverages you could do without.

Whether you should continue to shop for insurance after you have already purchased a policy depends on whether you live in a small town or a large metropolitan area. Small-town agents tend to work harder to keep your business. Because there is a limited pool of clients to draw from, they will make an effort to keep your premiums low. In a larger city, your agent may treat you with less of a personal touch, so you may not be getting the best deal from your agent.

One thing that insurance companies could do to help lower rates overall is to implement more thorough investigations of both potential policyholders and insurance agents. Fraud occurs both on the consumer level and the agent level, and undetected fraud costs all policyholders money in the form of higher premiums.

CASE STUDY: JUDY C.

One of the most important things that has helped my husband and me reduce the amounts we pay for insurance has been to carry all of our insurance policies with the same company. We have our home, auto, and life insurance through the same agent. We get discounts for having all three policies with the same company and receive additional discounts the longer we keep our policies with that agent.

Some people prefer to call direct writers, but I have had a better experience working with a personal agent. You can sit down face to face with an agent, and he or she will tell you about ways to save money on your insurance policies. Recently, my agent told me how I could save money on an automobile loan by financing my car through the company's program.

One thing you should do before you begin gathering quotes is to talk to people who live in your area to gather their opinions on local agents. You will quickly find out which agents are helpful and trustworthy, and which ones are only concerned about making commissions.

The most important thing you can do to help you save money on your insurance rates is to review your finances to see how much risk you can bear. If you have the money available to meet a high deductible, you will benefit in the form of lower premiums.

CASE STUDY: KELLY A.

Columbus, Ohio

One of the best ways I have found for saving money on insurance is to make sure you can find an agent or company you can trust. A trustworthy agent will help you find ways to cut your insurance premiums, such as using discounts you may not have thought of.

Also, using a direct writer for some types of insurance, such as automobile insurance, can be helpful. Direct writers often do not have to pay the huge overhead expenses of individual agent offices, so they can often pass the savings along to you in the form of lower premiums. Many people are hesitant to use direct writers, thinking they are for high-risk drivers, but increased competition has forced direct writers to offer better service, better coverages, and enhanced claims handling.

One thing that state insurance departments could do to help lower premiums would be to further deregulate the rating practices of insurance companies. Competition will help to lower rates where strict regulation will not. Consumers need to have access to a competitive insurance market so they will be able to find insurance through the company that operates most efficiently and therefore is able to offer the lowest rates while maintaining the ability to pay claims.

CASE STUDY: JOHN J.

Columbus, Ohio

In my experience, I have been able to save money on insurance by maintaining a responsible life style. Keeping a clean driving record, keeping your home well repaired and sidewalks free of cracks and debris, and maintaining good health are activities that will have a lasting impact on your insurance premiums.

In Ohio, insurance rates have slowly but steadily risen over the past five years; however, companies in the auto insurance market seem to be reducing rates in an effort to gain market share. We have entered a soft market nationwide, so there are more insurers competing for the same customers. As a consumer, you can use this to your advantage by shopping more aggressively for auto insurance.

One of the most important things a consumer can do to save money is to shop around. Insurance companies change their rates frequently, especially for home and auto insurance, so even if you started out at a cheap rate, you may be surprised at renewal. Always keep an eye on insurance company advertisements to see which companies have recently lowered their insurance rates.

CASE STUDY: ERNESTO S.

Johnstown, Ohio

One of the most important things you can do to save money on personal insurance is to thoroughly understand what you are buying. Many consumers rely on an agent to tell them what they need — although this is an easy solution, agents will often sell whatever will bring in the highest commission, rather than what the customer needs.

Educating yourself about insurance is also important because your agent may neglect to ask you if you need a particular type of coverage, especially if the coverage is not common. If you have a loss that a coverage would have paid for, you may be left wondering why your agent did not offer you the coverage. Do not wait on your agent to tell you what you need — use the Internet to find information on what coverages are available and why you may need each one. If your agent or your company cannot offer you the coverage, find another agent.

Overall, you are likely to see a decrease in personal rates over the next five years, particularly for property and casualty insurance lines. There are more companies competing for your business, especially if you are in the high-risk market. The only effective way the companies can obtain and keep your business is by finding ways to lower premium rates.

CASE STUDY: JON P. DIAMOND

Safe Auto Insurance Company
3883 East Broad Street
Columbus, Ohio 43213
1 (800) Safe-Auto

Rather than simply focusing on obtaining "cheap" insurance, I, and most of SafeAuto's customers, look for affordable car insurance that provides the best value and coverage for each of our unique circumstances. SafeAuto is always looking to offer the best price that meets the customers' auto insurance and risk protection needs.

This is where licensed insurance sales professionals play a crucial role in working with consumers to make sure they have the right coverage. The purpose of insurance is to protect a person's assets in the event he or she is found liable in a loss. So each individual has to determine how much protection he or she needs based on his or her financial situation. In the event customers do not have assets beyond the state

CASE STUDY: JON P. DIAMOND

minimum limits of liability, they purchase our minimum coverage so they are in compliance with the various state financial responsibility laws. "Full coverage" or physical damage and theft coverage is optional.

I am not sure anyone can tell if they have found the lowest insurance rate. Unlike most tangible products, insurance prices are unique to each individual's circumstance — there is no such thing as one price fits all. That is the reason it is important to deal with a company like SafeAuto, who has licensed representatives that specialize in auto insurance. SafeAuto's licensed insurance professionals help ensure they have all the pertinent information to give you the best coverage at the best rate — including discounts.

To obtain the best rate possible, have the basic information about your automobile (year, make, and model) and the Vehicle Identification Number, or VIN, available. Also be ready to accurately answer how many accidents and violations you have had and when — this will be verified through the state bureaus of motor vehicles. More important is what kind of car you drive: Is it new, old, in good condition, a sports car (large engine), or have a high theft rate?

Here are a few more tips for saving money on your car insurance:

- Keep your driver's record clean and up to date. Drive carefully and obey all applicable laws. The greater frequency of tickets and accidents, the higher your insurance costs will be.

- Do not have lapses in your coverage, and try to have proof of prior insurance — these are the main reasons people are in the nonstandard market to begin with.

- Consider higher deductibles if you can afford them.

- Drive a "low profile" car (not a high-powered sports car) equipped with money-saving safety features.

- Consider insuring with the state required level of insurance if you do not have assets exceeding that amount.

- Make sure you get all discounts for which you qualify.

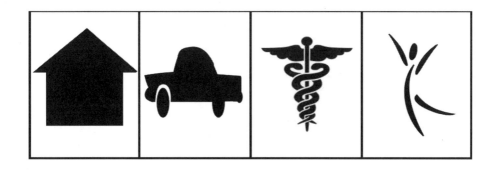

BIBLIOGRAPHY

Baldwin, Ben G. *The New Life Insurance Advestment Advisor, 2nd Ed.* New York, NY: McGraw-Hill Publishing Co., 2002

Hondros Editors. *Ohio Life and Health Licensing Textbook.* Columbus, OH: Hondros College/P.I.S., 2001

Hunglemann, Jack. *Insurance for Dummies.* Hoboken, NJ: Wiley Publishing, Inc., 2001

National Association of Insurance Commissioners, **www.naic.org**

Pilzer, Paul Z. *The New Health Insurance Solution.* Hoboken, NJ: John Wiley & Sons, Inc., 2005

The Silver Lake Editors. *Hassle-Free Health Coverage.* Los Angeles, CA: Silver Lake Publishing, 1999

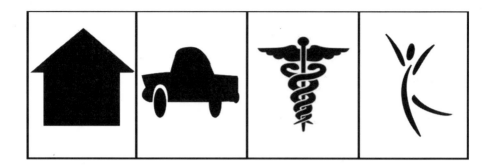

AUTHOR BIOGRAPHY

Carla and Lee Rowley are professional writers who have more than a decade of experience in the personal insurance industry. Carla has spent years with a national multiline insurance company, working to ensure that policyholders obtain the appropriate coverages at the best prices for both commercial and personal lines. Lee has spent years building the regulatory compliance division of a growing personal lines insurance company, working with state regulators on key issues affecting the insurance-buying public.

When not working to serve the needs of insurance consumers, Carla and Lee run Java Joint Media, a full-service copywriting firm that provides Web site content and print copy for a variety of international clients. To learn more, visit **www.javajointmedia.com**.

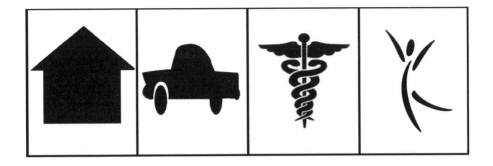

INDEX